Rainy Day
Horsemanship

Also by Vanessa Bee

The Horse Agility Handbook

3-Minute Horsemanship

Over, Under, Through: Obstacle Training for Horses

Horse Agility (streaming video)

Rainy Day Horsemanship

50 EXERCISES

TO DO WITH YOUR HORSE
WHEN YOU CAN'T RIDE

VANESSA BEE

TRAFALGAR SQUARE
North Pomfret, Vermont

First published in 2023 by
Trafalgar Square Books
North Pomfret, Vermont 05053

Disclaimer of Liability
The author and publisher shall have neither liability nor responsibility to any person or entity with respect to any loss or damage caused or alleged to be caused directly or indirectly by the information contained in this book. While the book is as accurate as the author can make it, there may be errors, omissions, and inaccuracies.

Trafalgar Square Books encourages the use of approved safety helmets in all equestrian sports and activities.

Library of Congress Cataloging-in-Publication Data

Names: Bee, Vanessa, author.
Title: Rainy day horsemanship : 50 exercises to do with your horse when you
  can't ride / Vanessa Bee.
Description: North Pomfret : Trafalgar Square Books, 2023. | Includes index. |
  Summary: "Clever ways to improve your horse's performance when groundwork is all you can do. There are dozens of reasons you might not be able to ride your horse. Weather can have an impact on your riding and training choices, sometimes keeping you out of the saddle, as can an injury to you or your horse, or changes in lifestyle or horsemanship goals. But time not riding does not need to be time wasted, explains trainer and popular instructor Vanessa Bee. As Founder of the International Horse Agility Club, Bee brings to the stable a unique set of skill-building techniques and exercises that anyone can use to better understand how the horse moves and how to influence that movement, resulting in better behavior on the ground, improved performance under saddle, and strengthened connection whenever and however you and your horse interact"-- Provided by publisher.
Identifiers: LCCN 2023014836 (print) | LCCN 2023014837 (ebook) | ISBN 9781646011919 (paperback) |
  ISBN 9781646011926 (epub)
Subjects: LCSH: Horses--Training.
Classification: LCC SF287 .B3695 2023 (print) | LCC SF287 (ebook) | DDC 636.1/0835--dc23/eng/20230504
LC record available at https://lccn.loc.gov/2023014836LC ebook record available at https://lccn.loc.gov/2023014837

Photos by Vanessa Bee
Book design by Lauryl Eddlemon
Cover design by RM Didier

Printed in China

10 9 8 7 6 5 4 3 2 1

DEDICATION

For Secret, my friend and teacher, thank you.
May 1, 1995 – September 17, 2022

Contents

58
EXERCISE 13
63
EXERCISE 16
93
EXERCISE 25

104
EXERCISE 28
108
EXERCISE 30
152
EXERCISE 47

What Is Rainy Day Horsemanship?

It was one of those days guaranteed to keep humans and their horses indoors. Rain thundered against the barn as I sprinted from my car under an umbrella that really wasn't doing a great job of keeping me dry. I opened the door and splashed my way into the barn aisle.

The horse nearest the door snorted and pushed against the back wall of his stall, eyes rolling.

"He hates umbrellas," said Nancy, one of my students. "That's why I got such a rotten dressage score last week. Started to rain and everyone put up their umbrellas."

"Sorry." I carefully closed the umbrella, trying not to make too much noise or spray everyone with raindrops. Propped in the corner, it proceeded to create an impressive puddle.

My students were sitting on hay bales looking gloomily at each other.

"What are we going to do? We're bored, our horses are bored, we can't go out in this. You've had a wasted journey."

I looked around the barn. It had the usual storage areas with poles, blankets, cones, and buckets tidily packed away.

"Not wasted at all," I announced. "Today you're all going to improve your dressage scores."

There were groans and mumbles about not going out in the wet, certainly not riding, and definitely not getting their expensive saddles wet.

"You don't need to go out and you don't need a saddle. All you need is a horse with a halter and lead rope. Today, you're going to have some fun. And here's your first toy."

I picked up the closed umbrella. My students were looking at me curiously now.

"Nancy's horse is frightened of umbrellas. Let's help him understand that they are quite safe. What worries the rest of your horses when you go out?" I looked round at the group. Their answers quickly came back.

"Those mats they sometimes put down to stop the arena gateways getting slippery."

"Flags on the way to the arena."

"The white dressage boards around the ring."

"Narrow gateways and corridors at the showgrounds."

"Just leading him through a crowd at a show!"

"Well, that's a good start," I announced. "We'll need some feed bags tied onto sticks, a couple of old horse blankets, two barrels, a pole or two, and my umbrella. We're going to do some 'Rainy Day Horsemanship.'"

And that's exactly what we did.

AND WHAT HAPPENED NEXT?

That small group of students grew into many groups of students, and I quickly collected a lot of common "problems" that people experience with their horses and started to help solve them without any of us even needing to leave the barn.

I began writing down some notes and plans to help people remember the ideas, and before long, I realized I had the makings of a book that people might find useful when they couldn't ride. Of course, I didn't want the photographs to be all blue skies and sunshine. I needed to show real people, coping with real rainy weather! However, the summer I worked on the book was one of the driest, hottest, sunniest summers for nearly 50 years. Day after day, the sun blazed down from a cloudless blue sky. Our problem wasn't rain and wind, it was heat and flies—and guess what? Working on our "rainy day" exercises in the cool, shady barn was a relief. So be assured that while many of the photos in these pages are taken in blazing sunshine rather than in the rain, the lessons apply, whatever the weather!

Then, Carol, a friend who had agreed to help with the photos, badly injured her leg, quite unconnected with her handling horses. She was scrambling up a bank with her new puppy when she slipped on the wet grass. There was a nasty cracking sound, her leg wasn't the shape it should have been, and Carol found herself confined to a wheelchair for a week before she was able to wear a leg brace and then eventually

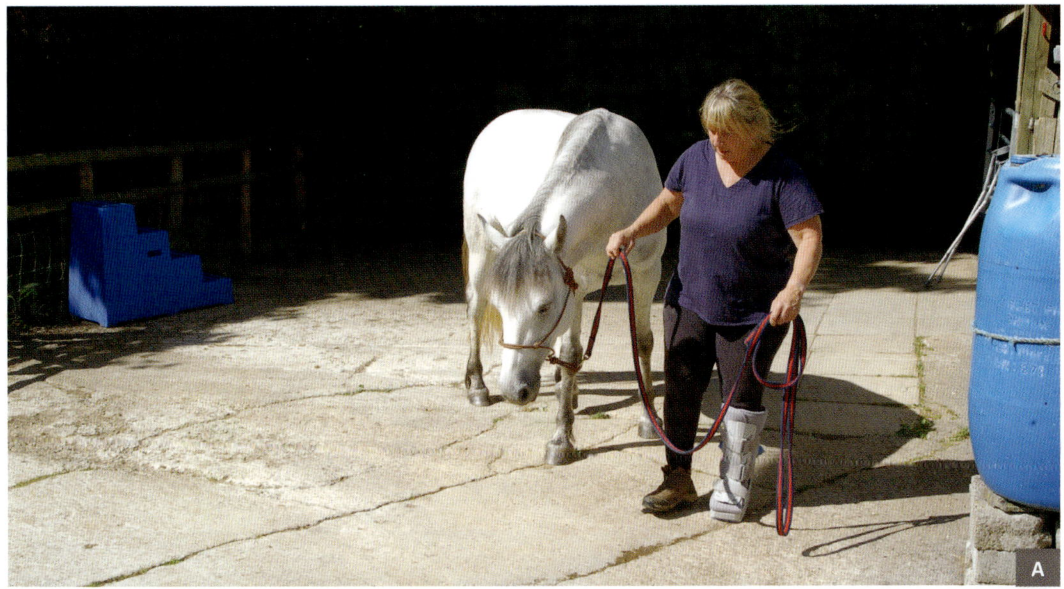

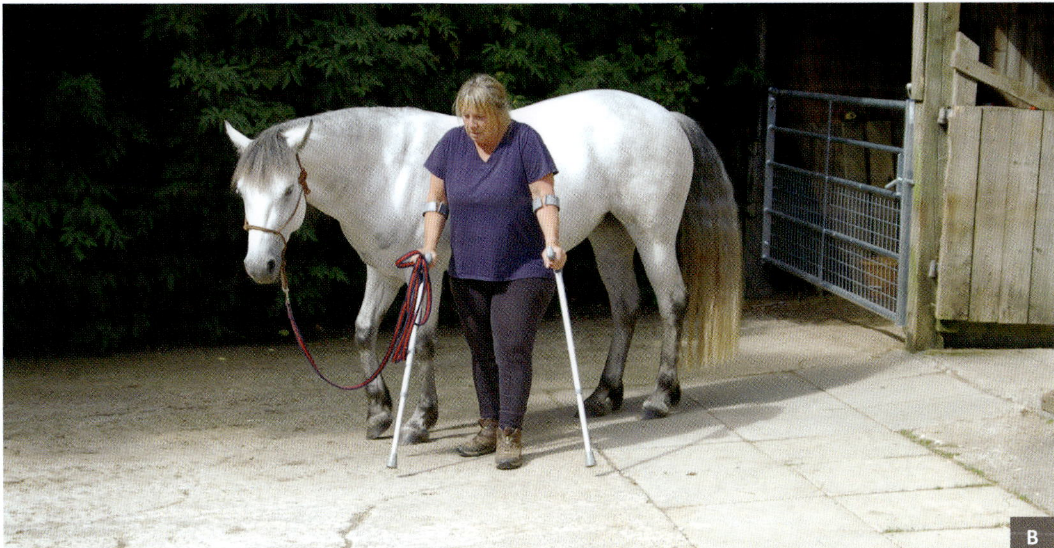

I.1A & B Carol found her leg brace made walking difficult, but her horse Melody soon got used to walking slowly and carefully beside her (A). When Carol moved on to crutches, she really had to think about how to safely hold the lead rope (B).

move about on crutches (figs. I.1A & B). Despite all this, she was able to continue looking after her own horses; she had done so much groundwork and obstacle training with them, using some of the very exercises I teach in this book, they just saw it just another game.

And then my own equine partner, Secret, who helped me with the photographs in all my previous books, sustained a very nasty knee injury in the field. When she was transfered to an equine hospital, I began to realize that she would probably be confined in a small space for some time. I felt a sense of irony that I should be writing a book about the very exercises I knew would be invaluable to keep her entertained while she recovered. It gave me hope that all would come right in the end. However, it wasn't to be. Secret

GROUNDWORK TO BUILD CONFIDENCE

Nearly 30 years ago, I rehabilitated a very traumatized Arabian mare. We spent months working on the ground before I rode her, and you'll find many of the things I did to reach that point in this book. When at last she felt ready to be ridden, it was a real triumph for me, but it was not all fair sailing.

In the early days of being ridden, the mare would often stop, throw her head up, and panic. I got pretty good at kicking my feet out of the stirrups and jumping down. I always had a long rope attached to a halter under the bridle so I was immediately able to feel safe because I knew, after months of work, I could handle her on the ground. Each time this happened the look of relief on that horse was instant. It was as if she was saying, "Thank goodness you're here. Something scary just happened and I need your help."

I had spent so much time on the ground with her that it gave me the confidence to do this—I felt braver and that, in turn, rubbed off on the horse. Those emergency dismounts became fewer and fewer until eventually I was able to ride long distances without a panic in sight.

could not survive the injuries; I had to make the heartbreaking decision to let her go.

But the extreme heat of that summer, the injury to my friend, and the worry that I could have a horse on stall rest for a long time all had made me realize that Rainy Day Horsemanship isn't just about "not going riding because the weather is bad." It is about preparing your horse to accept all manner of changes that could happen to him, to you, and to the world around you both. The weather can keep you inside, one of you could be injured and have limited mobility for a while, or you might decide you prefer to do things with your horse other than riding. Your time with your horse need not be wasted. The simple exercises that follow need little space or equipment and are designed to develop a strong relationship between you and your horse, as well as help you both become more able to cope with life outside your barn.

Making a great ridden horse doesn't start from the saddle, it starts from the ground, and that is why you don't need to ride to get a better riding horse or become a better rider. A day not riding is not a wasted day; it's an opportunity to learn more about how a horse moves and how to encourage him to move in the way you want him to.

HOW TO USE THIS BOOK

I have written this book so you can dip into it easily, without working through from cover to cover; however, I do suggest you turn all the pages first so that you can familiarize yourself with the exercises before choosing a place to begin. Some of you may already have a lot of horsemanship knowledge and will be able to dive straight into the more complex lessons, but do be aware that your horse, unless you've had him a long time and know him well, may have a few hidden fears that just haven't shown up yet. If you start right at the beginning of the book, you can just do a quick check that he's okay with the "small stuff" before you challenge him later.

As I've said, these exercises aren't just for when there's inclement weather, so you can work on them in a paddock or arena whenever it is possible. If you are forced indoors, you don't need a big space to complete these exercises. With most, a stall or the barn aisle will give you plenty of room to work. You don't need an indoor arena.

The book is split into three sections:

- Part One—It's All About the Horse!
- Part Two—It's All About You!
- Part Three—50 Exercises for a Rainy Day

Part Three is divided into six subsections (note that while I've used weather-related terminology to help categorize the lessons, it of course isn't always going to be literal—choose what makes sense for your and your horse's needs on that particular day):

- **Drizzling:** 4 short, simple exercises to get you started.
- **Cloudburst:** 6 exercises to practice your safe handling skills when a "sudden heavy rainstorm" spoils your plans to go outside.
- **Showery:** 14 ways to build a trusting relationship with your horse when "the rain showers just keep rolling through."
- **Downpour:** 13 fun things to do when "the rain never seems to stop."
- **Thunderstorm:** 9 challenging exercises to keep your mind off "the thunder and lightning."
- **The Sun Is Shining!** 4 ways to put the lessons you've learned to the test.

PART ONE

It's All About the Horse!

What does every horse need to live a comfortable, fulfilled life?

Animal behaviorists have devised a list called The Five Domains (or Freedoms), which covers animal welfare. The first three items are: the right food for the animal's lifestyle and fresh water available at all times; comfort in his environment with shelter from the weather and space to move around; and freedom from pain.

These three are all easy for us to manage with our horses, but the final two items on the list state that the animal must be allowed to express himself and not feel afraid. I'd like you to pause and think about this. Do you give your horse the freedom to express himself in the ways that horses do toward other horses? Does he have the chance to interact with other horses to enable him to have this opportunity? And with you, for example, if his tail swishes or he nips when you're grooming him?

Think about wild horses. They are free to express themselves and are very good at telling other horses what they like and don't like. With no pressure to do anything other than horsey things, like grazing and snoozing, they have time to interact with other herd members. They don't constantly spook and run away if something frightens them; they have time to examine it first, and within their own learning pattern, approach and learn if the scary thing really is that bad. They can't waste energy spooking and running; they need to save it for when they really need it.

Do you allow your horse free time in an enriching environment to explore and learn without interruption or guidance from you?

You have a domestic horse who was untamed when he was born, but then trained by humans so he can live in a human world. I prepare a lot of wild horses for a domestic lifestyle, and I like to teach them what I call the *Five Foundation Skills:* Catching, Leading, Tying, Foot Handling and Loading.

I believe that a well-prepared domestic horse should be completely fluent in these Five Foundation Skills, whatever his role in domesticity. Many of the "problems" I'm asked to help solve would simply never have happened if the horse had been trained thoroughly in each of these five skills. How fluent is *your* horse in the Five Foundation Skills?

1 CATCHING

Strange, isn't it, that we say we're going to "catch our horse"? We'd never say that we're going to "catch our dog" and take him for walk. Let's change that mindset. I like to call it "picking up." Actually, I don't go and "pick him up"—my horse comes to me. I go out to the pasture and whistle, and in he comes at a gallop. There's no magic there; I've associated my whistle with feeding time, so no matter how far away he is, if I whistle, my horse comes to me.

My three ponies were all "uncatch-able" in a large space when they first came to live with me. So, I trained them first

to come to the whistle for food in a small space, and then I "caught" them in there. I never did anything other than put the halter on and give them a bit of a stroke and scratch. I made putting the halter on a nice experience.

Now, when I go out into an open space and call them, the ponies are happy to come and for me to put the halter on because it has pleasant associations. If, every time you "catch your horse," you work him hard or do something he isn't comfortable with, he'll soon decide that coming to you isn't going to lead to a pleasurable experience. Sometimes, you just need to pick him up from the field, and give him a bit of positive attention, then let him go.

2 LEADING

If a horse is good to lead, he is a joy to be with. A horse that needs to be pulled and pushed along is not—it's hard work for both the human and horse. Pulling on a horse's halter creates pressure around his head, and horses are programmed by nature to pull against any pressure and try to escape. When there is any tension on the lead rope, most horses just get slower and slower as they pull against that tension. You need to help the horse understand that he must *give* to pressure, and this takes patience and time. Every time you ask the horse to move, you need to feel the moment he starts to move, and stop asking. It really is that simple, and *timing* is the key here. You are not looking for huge movements, just a feeling that the horse is starting to move. If you keep the pressure on once he's started moving, he'll just pull away from that pressure.

3 TYING

I'm lucky that I rarely have to tie my horses, but it is a skill most horse owners will need if they are in a busy stable or want to go out to shows and clinics where horses need to be tied in a public space. Standing tied is very closely aligned to leading—it's all about the horse giving to the pressure of the lead rope, which in this case is tied to something solid rather than being attached to a human who is moving about.

4 FOOT HANDLING

I am always amazed at the number of domestic horses who will not stand still for even the simplest foot care. In some cases, there may be a past traumatic experience, or pain when the foot is lifted, such as a back injury, but usually, I see two reasons why the horse doesn't stand still to have his feet picked up:

- The horse has not been positioned with all four feet underneath him so when a foot is lifted, he can balance on the other three. By watching your horse, you can begin to see what he looks like when he's standing balanced over all four quarters. Try gently rocking his weight off one foot to make it easy to pick up.
- The horse has never been taught to pick his feet up. For a horse to willingly allow his feet to be picked up by a human takes a great deal of trust because a horse cannot run away from danger in this position.

5 TRAILER LOADING

You don't need to have a horse trailer to practice loading your horse in one. A trailer is made up of three construction elements: a floor, a roof, and the sides. From my experience, all horses have a concern about one of these. Some don't like walking over a change of surface, like a trailer ramp or floor; some don't like the low roof near their ears; and some really don't like the feeling of being squeezed into a tight space. You can work on these issues individually. Walk your horse over tarpaulins or safe wooden boards. Construct a simple tunnel to walk through, made of four jump wings arranged in a square with a tarpaulin draped over them to form a roof. Barrels can be lined up to create a narrow space to squeeze through. When the horse is comfortable with all three elements, you can start to put them all together. The barrels go on the board "floor," and the tarpaulin "roof" goes over the top of it all.

Even when I have a trailer available, I always work with these three elements separately first. It's so much safer than starting with a trailer, which can have sharp edges, hooks, and trip hazards.

START WITH THE "WILD" HORSE WITHIN

Whenever I help someone with a "problem" horse, I ignore the domestication that he's received, look for the "wild" horse within, and start there. The development of the handled horse from birth right through to old age depends on reading the horse and having the knowledge of how to mold the behaviors to make him safe and happy, both on the ground and when he's ridden.

It takes time to get to know an individual horse and it takes time to "read" a horse. Is he happy? How does he show pain? How does he look when he's content? How does he show his fear? What does he do when he gets scared? So many questions! In this book, I want to help you read your horse, understand his motivations, and know what to do when the two of you seem to be on different planets.

PART TWO

It's All About YOU!

It isn't just the horse's job to get good around a human; the human has to get good around horses! I have found that horses are much more adaptable than humans. If some things in this section make you feel a little uncomfortable, I urge you to be *interested* in that discomfort. Learning can be a very uncomfortable sensation! I encourage you to be interested in how you react to some of the ideas I throw your way. They're only suggestions. They work for me and my students, and they may work for you too.

I have a very great friend, Perry Wood, a classical equitation trainer who has helped me enormously with my riding skills. Many years ago, I was bemoaning the fact that I would never be able to ride like him. He said this, which has stayed with me always: "Vanessa, you will never ride like me. You will ride like Vanessa Bee, and that is more important than anything else."

The horse doesn't want to see us trying to be someone else; he wants to see us being the best that we can be. And the only way we can do that is to have the confidence to look at new ideas and decide if they can help us, and continually build our knowledge by watching, listening, and handling horses—lots of them.

THE ATTITUDE OF THE HANDLER

We hear a lot these days about being positive, mindful, and having the "right" attitude. But what does all this mean to you and your horse?

Here are some searching questions I ask my students, and I've put in a few of the answers I often receive, as well. There's no wrong or right or good or bad in this. No one is judging anyone here. I would like you just to consider how comfortable you feel about being asked the following questions in the first place, and what your own replies might be.

WHY DO YOU WANT TO BE AROUND HORSES?

- *Because I love them.*
- *Because I can't keep away from them.*
- *Because they win prizes for me.*
- *Because it's my hobby.*
- *Because my mother wants me to ride.*

WHAT DO YOU HAVE TO OFFER YOUR HORSE?

- *Love.*
- *Money and the best care.*
- *I'm a good rider.*
- *Lots of treats.*

WHAT DOES THE HORSE OFFER YOU? (This question always takes the longest to think through to an answer.)

- *Love.*
- *Companionship.*
- *Friendship.*
- *Prizes.*
- *Escape.*

ARE YOU PATIENT?

- *Yes!*
- *Sometimes, but not when he won't stand still or won't be caught.*

ARE YOU PHYSICALLY FIT?

- *No, I'm overweight.*
- *I haven't got time to exercise.*

ARE YOU EMOTIONALLY FIT?

- *That's a big question.*
- *I get frustrated when my horse doesn't do what I want.*
- *I get angry at myself when I get frustrated with my horse.*
- *Sometimes I smack my horse when I'm cross.*

HOW CONFIDENT ARE YOU AROUND HORSES?

- *I don't trust some of them.*
- *I'm only confident with my own horse.*
- *I get scared easily because I got badly kicked once.*

BEGINNING WITH THE RIGHT MINDSET

When I go out to help people with their horses, I often travel hundreds of miles to get to them. I dislike being late for these appointments because I feel that the person will already be anxious about my visit, and I don't want to add to their stress by being late. If I get stuck in traffic, I can feel my agitation growing, which is not really going to help the situation when I arrive. So I've devised a very short meditation that I practice before I go near *any* horse, including my own. When I first started doing this, it could take five or ten minutes to work, but now it's like a trigger—the moment I sit and visualize a still-burning candle flame, I am instantly calm. I have reproduced how I use the image of a candle flame on this page. Some people find this difficult, but I can assure you that when you do allow your heart, your mind, and your spirit to be still, your horse will know.

Why do you think so many horse people practice meditation and martial arts? You don't need to make a big thing of it; just "be still inside" when approaching and moving among horses, and they will reflect your stillness.

THE CANDLE FLAME MEDITATION

Here is my short mediation for you to try:

1. Sit upright but be comfortable and soft in your posture. You can close your eyes if you wish, but this isn't always possible or even necessary.

2. Think about your breathing.

3. If you need to move, be smooth in your movements.

4. Imagine a long white candle in a candle holder. Picture yourself lighting that candle. See the flame catch on the wick and grow tall and thin. Around the wick, the flame is clear, then it glows into yellows and whites. The edges of that flame shimmer in the heat. The flame is strong, and with your regular breathing, it stays strong; it does not waver or move about, but burns quietly, strongly, moving smoothly. No breeze changes its quietness.

5. Feel the stillness within you, strong, smooth, peaceful.

Of course, you can use your own visualization. My students have imagined being on a beach with white sands and a lapping blue lagoon. Others have imagined sitting in a garden looking at a single rose. Find out what works for you. No one needs to know what it is you imagine; it is between you and your horse.

ALWAYS KEEP LEARNING

My other suggestion is that you learn, explore, and expand your horsemanship knowledge. Read books, watch videos, listen to people talk about horses, then make your own decisions. This horsemanship journey is two individuals traveling together—you and your horse. There will be other travelers who will offer advice, so consider if that advice will help and enhance your present path, and if it won't, keep moving in the direction you feel is right for you. Your horse will thank you for it.

GETTING TO KNOW YOUR HORSE WHEN IT'S DRIZZLING

LEARNING SAFE HANDLING TECHNIQUES IN A CLOUDBURST

BUILDING A TRUSTING RELATIONSHIP WHEN IT'S SHOWERY

FUN THINGS TO TRY IN A DOWNPOUR

CHALLENGES TO FACE IN A THUNDERSTORM

DOING MORE—PUTTING SKILLS TO THE TEST IN THE OUTSIDE WORLD WHEN THE SUN IS SHINING

WHAT'S IN EACH EXERCISE

For each exercise:

- I explain **What** it is all about.
- Then, I give you a few ideas on **How** to make it happen, just in case you don't know where to start.
- But **What If** it just isn't working? In the last part of each entry, I guide you through a few troubleshooting ideas that have worked for me.

Drizzling

EXERCISE 1
Watching

WHAT IT IS

This may seem an odd thing to ask you to do, as you probably look at your horse a lot. You look for signs of ill health, see if he's too hot or cold or if he's moving well or not, then decide if you need to do something about it. In this exercise, I'm going ask you to just sit and watch your horse without making decisions about what you're going to do next. This is really asking you to be absolutely in the present, in the moment. You aren't looking for anything, *you are just watching.*

1 I watch my horses a lot; they are quite used to me hanging around them.

In this frantic world I feel too few of us take time to just observe without judgment, without a time limit, without thinking that we're wasting our time.

So this, your very first exercise, has very little instruction attached and it may take a lifetime to master. And for that reason, it is probably the most difficult exercise in the book.

HOW TO DO IT

Find yourself a comfortable place where you can just sit and observe your horse—ideally not too close to him because you want to see what he does when he's just hanging out in his stall or shed (fig. 1).

Sitting quietly and still, just watch your horse. It doesn't matter if he's eating, looking out over the door, or having a nap, just observe him. You will find that within seconds your mind will wander away to think about dinner or whether that mark on your horse's leg was there yesterday, or why your horse is behaving in a particular way. Don't worry, be interested in where your mind wandered off to, and then bring it back.

This is mindfulness, and I believe horses do this most of the time when they are left to their own devices. When they graze, doze, or walk over long distances to find water, that's all they are doing. They're not thinking about tomorrow's competition or yesterday's ride; they are just grazing, dozing, or walking. Of course, they can be distracted by outside stimuli, but in each moment they graze, they are just chewing. That is all they are doing—picking at grass, chewing, swallowing, and moving on.

Sit still and think like a horse.

WHAT IF

Most of us find this exercise very challenging. Don't beat yourself up if you can't even do two or three seconds without your mind going off to the market to buy dinner. This is not a competition even with yourself, it's just another way of getting inside your horse's mind so that you can understand him better.

There's no right or wrong here. This exercise is about you—you, thinking more like a horse.

EXERCISE 2
Observing Something New

WHAT IT IS

What does your horse do when he encounters something new?

Let's say you're out for a ride and around the corner comes a person leading an elephant. (There could possibly be one or two of you reading this book who regularly meet an elephant, but for most of us, this unlikely event would be a completely new experience!) Do you know what your horse would do? Can you describe, second by second, the series of events that would occur if an elephant appeared?

Most people I asked this question of immediately replied that their horse would bolt.

"Which way?" I ask.

They look bewildered. "Away from the elephant, of course!"

Then I begin to ask for more information about that bolt: "Would he throw his head up or down before he started to run? Which way would he turn? Would he spin on a front foot or a back foot? How long would he run before he slowed down, stopped, and looked back?"

I ask these and many more questions before some usually reply in an exasperated tone, "Does it matter? He just bolted to get away from the elephant."

I've chosen an extreme example here, but ask yourself, what does your horse do when he is afraid? If he always goes through the same series of signals, you can step in quickly before he gets to the running stage and help him calm down. In this exercise, you're going to find out what those signals are.

In some of the Rainy Day Horsemanship exercises ahead, you are going to ask the horse to do something he may never have done before—walk over a tarpaulin, for example. Some horses find this very worrying and will refuse to even *look* at the tarpaulin, let alone walk over it. So often, when this happens, the horse is labeled as "stubborn." I will say here and now that I have met many thousands of horses but never a stubborn one. However, I have met *a lot* of horses who refuse to do things when they are afraid.

2 A & B Ricky looks very confident as he marches toward the balloons (A), but he's ready to run if he needs to (B).

This exercise is about knowing what your horse looks and behaves like when he's just a bit anxious—not terrified out of his wits, but just a little concerned about something. So many wrecks wouldn't happen if only the person with a horse had noticed growing anxiety and reassured the horse instead of waiting until the animal is in full survival mode before trying to help him.

HOW TO DO IT

For this exercise you need to find something safe that your horse has never seen before. A child's pinwheel, a ball, or a flag, for example. Arrange the novel item so that the horse can see it and, from the moment you introduce it, observe the horse (figs. 2 A & B). There may be a fleeting reaction before he recognizes that the object isn't

scary, and he will then return to whatever he was doing before. Remember, you're not looking for a big reaction here, but instead to see what subtle signals might occur *before* he becomes really afraid.

What does he do when you introduce the "scary" object? Does he stare at it? Or just glance at it and immediately walk away? Don't try and influence his decision. As long as you have selected the item carefully, he will be in no danger.

This isn't a training exercise for your horse or a competition; it's just you observing what your horse does when he's a bit worried about something. Remember, once he's trying to run away from it, there is too much fear. You've either chosen something too frightening, or it's been introduced too

WHAT FEAR LOOKS LIKE

I used to think I knew what fear looked like in a horse. It was nearly 30 years ago that all that changed when I bought an unhandled pony named Russet. I had purchased his brother, and the owner offered Russet for a knock-down price. I had an empty space in the trailer, so in went Russet alongside my new driving pony.

It was only when I got them home that I realized I was completely out of my depth and knew nothing about the untrained pony. Russet could not be caught in an open field, and even when we got him inside a stall (by driving him with flags) it took quite some time to get a halter on him. He did not lead at all; he needed to be dragged to get going, and hauled to a stop. He would frequently pull away and run in a complete panic round the field.

It was ugly.

I had been round horses and ponies all my life, but I realized then I knew nothing about them. I knew about trained, domestic horses, not raw, unhandled ones. Every horse person I spoke to told me Russet was a danger to me and to others. "Just put him down."

And so I did.

I knew immediately that I'd missed something, that I'd made the wrong choice. It's so easy with the internet now to find someone, somewhere, anywhere in the world to help, but this was long before such resources were available. With the knowledge I have now, I know Russet wasn't dangerous.

Russet died because he was afraid.

Russet changed my life.

Until Russet, I only knew about domestic horses who presented the behaviors I expected to see. An untouched horse reacted in a completely different way—it was pure horse communication with no adjustments for humans. I needed to interact in a way I had never had to before; I needed to start to think and communicate like a horse if I was ever to understand them.

I set out to learn from as many people as I could, reading, watching videos, and traveling all over the world to clinicians who looked like they could help me learn. I was driven by a desire to never let another horse or pony die just because he was afraid.

quickly. You're only looking for the early signals your horse gives you that let you know he *might* make a run for his life! Some of these fear signals can be:

- A tight mouth.
- A droopy eyelid.
- Increased breath rate.
- Standing still and stiff in his body.
- Looking back over his shoulder (for an escape route).

These are a tiny selection of what you might see, but show you how very small fear signals can be. In *extreme fear,* the horse can resort to one of the "Four Fs":

- He can *flee,* which is what he would do in the open.
- He can *fight* when he's trapped in a small space.
- He can *freeze,* and I see this a lot. Just because a horse is standing still doesn't mean he's accepted the situation, he's just too scared to run. (Just an aside here, when a horse is standing still and resting his hind leg, it can mean he's in the "Ready, Steady, Go," position, and he'll kick off with that foot when he suddenly goes into flight.)
- He could *faint.* By this I mean the horse collapses in fear. It's not common, but I have seen it happen.

These are BIG reactions and not what you want to get near on a rainy day—or any day—at the barn!

WHAT IF

What do you do when your horse does nothing; there is absolutely no change in behavior? Well, first of all, are you being observant enough? Maybe he did make a tiny fear signal, but you missed it.

Is the scary object near enough? With some horses, they can see a small flag from across the field and panic, whereas others don't notice until the flag is much closer. Remember, you're not trying to deliberately scare the horse here, you're just seeing how he reacts in the first instant to something that is new in his environment.

EXERCISE 3
What Motivates Your Horse?

WHAT IT IS

Why does your horse do what you want him to do? It sounds like a strange question, but I've heard a lot of different answers:

- Because he's told to.
- Because he loves me.
- Because he loves to work.
- Because I feed him.
- Because I am his leader.
- Because he loves competitions and winning.

I'm not saying any of these are right or wrong, but it's the rare horse that will complete a dressage pattern or jump a course of jumps without a human being asking him to do so!

If you look back at the Five Freedoms (p. 7), you can see that a horse's needs include good nutrition, a suitable environment, health care, being able to behave naturally, and have a balanced mental state.

Let's assume your horse has a comfortable life where all these are satisfied:

- He receives the correct food for his workload and age.
- He has room to move around freely when not in work.
- His health is monitored to make sure he is kept free from disease and pain.
- He is allowed to express himself as a horse.
- His mental state is monitored because his owner listens to him when he says something isn't right.

When a horse has all these in place, what makes him want to come and do things with a human being? What motivates your horse? You are a responsible horse owner, and your horse has everything he needs. Why would he do anything as "unnatural" as pick up a hat and give it to his handler (for example)? This is where doing something constructive with your horse on a rainy day really comes into its own.

Horses get bored standing in a stall all day. When you look at the list

3 My ponies are motivated by food!

of requirements to give them a full life, standing still inside four walls with nothing to do isn't one of them. Yet we know there are times that this has to happen: extreme weather and stall rest, to name just two. Having something interesting to do will certainly help keep a horse "emotionally fit," so it is good to know what would motivate our horses to work with us.

HOW TO DO IT

Finding out what motivates your horse can take a long time, but here's a few suggestions:

- **Food**—Does he like treats, fruit, vegetables? Will he learn something new when given a food reward as he starts to understand and carry out the task (fig. 3)?

- **Scratches**—With some equines, food is not an option, but a good scratch in the right itchy place can really help a horse start looking for answers. Your job is to find that "sweet spot" (see Exercise 4, p. 28).

- **Rest**—This doesn't mean long periods of rest; it may just mean leaving the horse time to realize you are asking him to do something and give you an answer.

Let me write this again: *Ask and give him time to answer!* Just like humans, when we ask a horse to do something he needs to go through a process of:

- Knowing we're asking him to do something.
- Working out the answer.
- Delivering the answer.

When he gives you the answer you are looking for, you can give him food, a scratch, or just a rest. That is what this exercise is all about—finding out what motivates your horse.

WHAT IF

What do you do when your horse doesn't seem to be motivated by anything? What if you ask him to do something, and he just does nothing or says, "No"? You need to ask yourself why. Here are five possible reasons:

1. Is he afraid?

2. Does he understand the question?

3. Is he in pain?

4. Does he trust you?

5. Is he tired?

(Please note: "stubborn" and "naughty" are two words not on this list!)

The first thing to identify is which of these five reasons is relevant to the question you're asking. Let's work through an example: You ask a horse to walk through a pool of water, and he refuses to do so.

1. Is he afraid? Is it because he does not know how deep the water is or he has a fear of water because of previous experiences around it? Is there something he can see on

the other side of the pool—a scary log, for example?

2. Perhaps he doesn't understand why you want him to walk through water when there is a perfectly good way around it. It's not that he's afraid, he just doesn't understand the question. This is where your leading skills need to get really solid (see Exercise 9, *Easy Leading*, p. 43). Once that halter is on the horse, he needs to trust you're going to look after him wherever you ask him to go. This leads to the fourth question in this list (below).

3. Is he in pain? Could his feet hurt because the edge of the water is stony? Is there a steep bank to get into the water that is uncomfortable for him to climb down?

4. Does he trust you? If he doesn't trust your judgment that the water is safe, time spent indoors, working through constructive exercises, can only increase the bond between the two of you—not only does it increase his trust in you, but you really get to know him and trust him. (Note: You will begin to see the connection between the way he reacts to walking over a tarpaulin, which we do in Exercise 30, *Crossing a Tarpaulin*, p. 107, and walking through water because the two actions are so similar—that is, crossing a change in surface. By helping your horse understand that a change of surface is safe in the barn, you will improve your experience out on the trail.)

5. And the last reason he may not want to walk through the water is because he's just tired. Perhaps it's been a long trail ride, the water question is not heading toward home, and he doesn't have the energy to go any farther.

When your horse says, "No," go through this list of five questions, and identify why he doesn't want to do what you have asked him. When you have helped him achieve the task, you can increase the likelihood he will repeat it by giving him what motivates him—whether food, scratches, or rest.

EXERCISE 4
Finding the Horse's "Sweet Spot"

WHAT IT IS

Finding the place the horse loves to be scratched or rubbed can be a really good way to bond with your horse. In Exercise 3 (see p. 24), I talked about scratches being a motivator for some horses. The scratch does not need to be a great hefty scratch such as one horse gives another; sometimes a single long, firm stroke is enough. If you have a horse who is itchy—losing his winter coat, for example—you can really give him some pleasure (yes, I do mean pleasure) by finding that place he just can't reach himself and helping him alleviate the itch.

When I handle wild horses, I find that

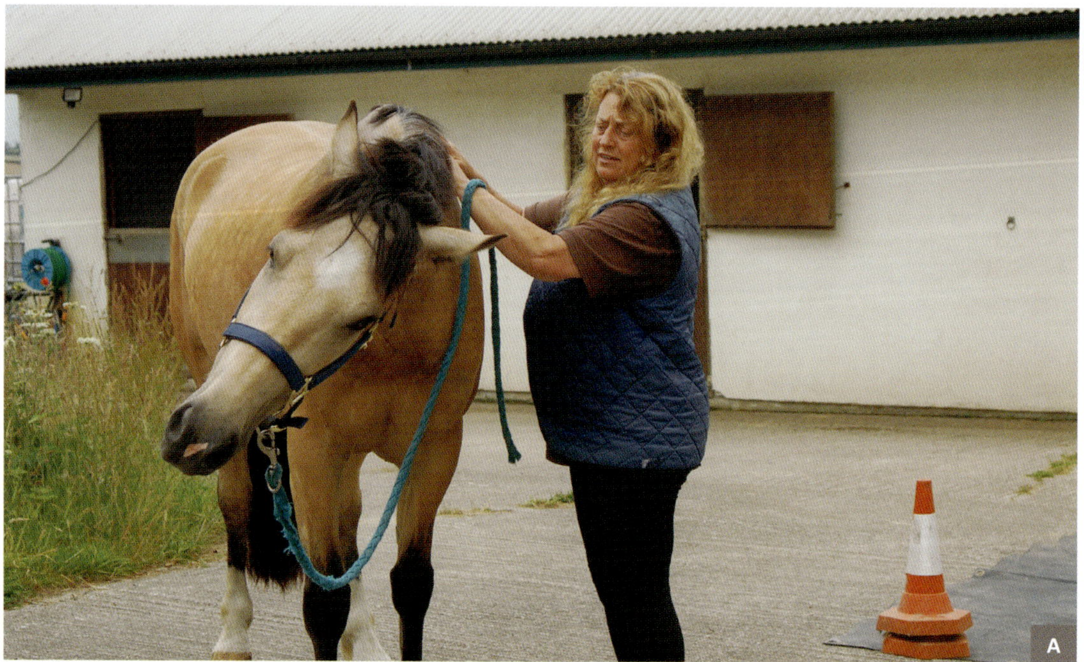

4 A & B Watch your horse carefully to make sure he's really enjoying those scratches (A). You need to know your horse well if you are going to work toward the hind end (B).

under the jaw is often a place I can help them out once I have a halter on them. I go from being somebody of little use to them to being a useful partner in helping them feel more comfortable.

HOW TO DO IT

Start on the horse's neck and shoulder with your fingers and rub the hair on the neck (fig. 4 A). If you have long nails, wearing gloves may be a good idea here. This is rubbing more than a scratch at first. Watch your horse's reaction. Remember Exercise 2, *Observing Something New* (p. 19). If he shows signs of fear or irritability, stop immediately because this may not be for him. Some horses do not like being touched at all, but you will probably already know this because of your horse's reaction when he is being groomed.

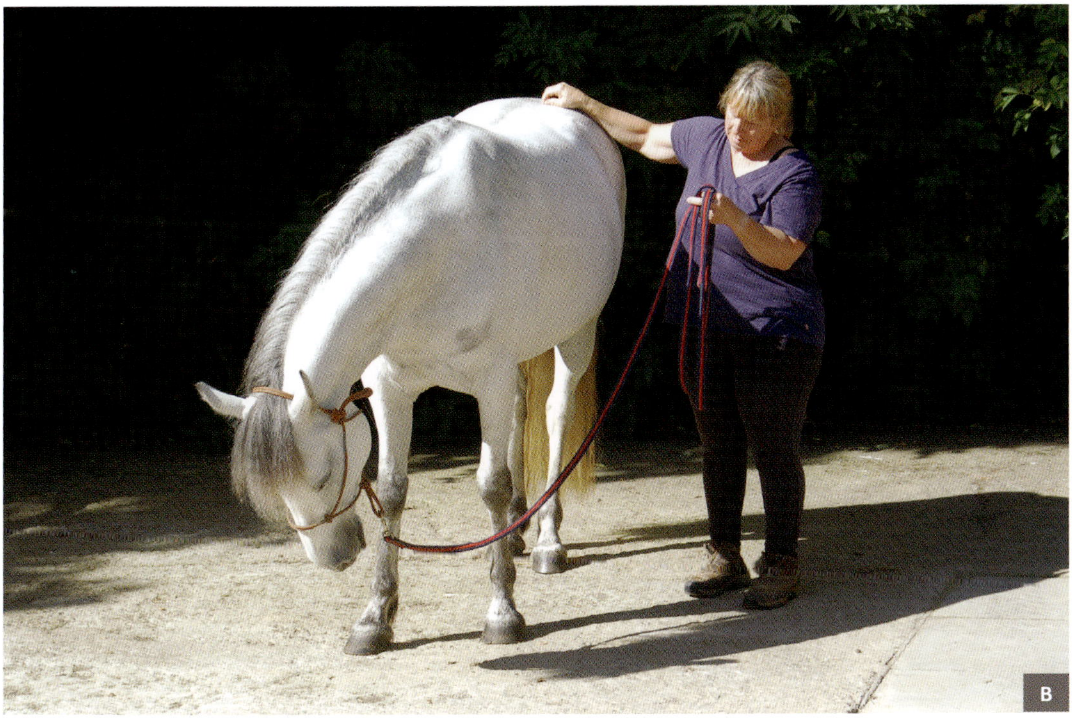

Move over the horse's body as you rub and watch his head position, mouth, and eyes. On most horses, you will reach a spot that causes them to twist their head around and move their lips as they enjoy the sensation.

WHAT IF

Remember, some horses do not like being touched. It might be, simply, that they just do not like the sensation, but there could other reasons. Think about the five reasons a horse doesn't behave as you want (see Exercise 3, *What Motivates Your Horse?*, p. 24). Ask yourself which reason could be relevant to this situation.

Be careful as you work over your horse's body, trying to find that itchy spot.

Watch his body language and look for those "Don't touch me there!" moments (fig. 4 B). Some horses will shift themselves around to get you in the right place. Take some time to observe horses in the field grooming each other and see how they move around to indicate to their friend where he needs to go next.

Just a word of warning here: when horses groom each other, they can be pretty rough. When you are giving your horse a scratch, be aware that he might start to groom you, too, and it can hurt as he rakes his teeth over your skin. Be careful of your reaction if this is the case, as he is showing he wants to bond with you, and if you object, he really won't understand why.

Cloudburst

EXERCISE 5
Haltering

WHAT IT IS

Let me ask you a question: how does a horse defend himself?

This is something I ask a lot of my students, and the answers range from "biting" to "kicking" to "making a charging attack." This may be true for a horse trapped in a small space, but let's just imagine he's out on the wide, open plain, and something attacks him—what does he do?

The horse defends himself by running away.

When we put a halter onto a horse, we take away his main means of defending himself, and that puts us in a huge position of trust. When the horse cannot defend himself, we need to be prepared to take on that responsibility.

If he gets scared, he may try to get away by pulling on the lead rope. If you are holding on tight, or he's tied up, he may start to move his feet a lot because he feels he needs to get away. He may barge into you, and bite or kick as he tries to escape. Many of us would get angry and tell him to behave himself, but that's exactly what he is doing—he is behaving himself as a horse does when he's uncomfortable in any situation. He's trying to escape.

HOW TO DO IT

Let's start at the beginning. How you put the halter on can make or break your day with your horse. Let's imagine that there he is, enjoying his morning hay, when his handler walks up to him, drags the halter on over his soft whiskery nose, catches his nostrils roughly, and pulls it over his eyes without care. For him, not a great way to start the day.

When I'm haltering my horses, I like to get their attention first (usually by blowing kisses at them!); then, when they raise their heads, I put my right arm over the neck and my left under the neck. The left hand is holding the poll strap of the halter.

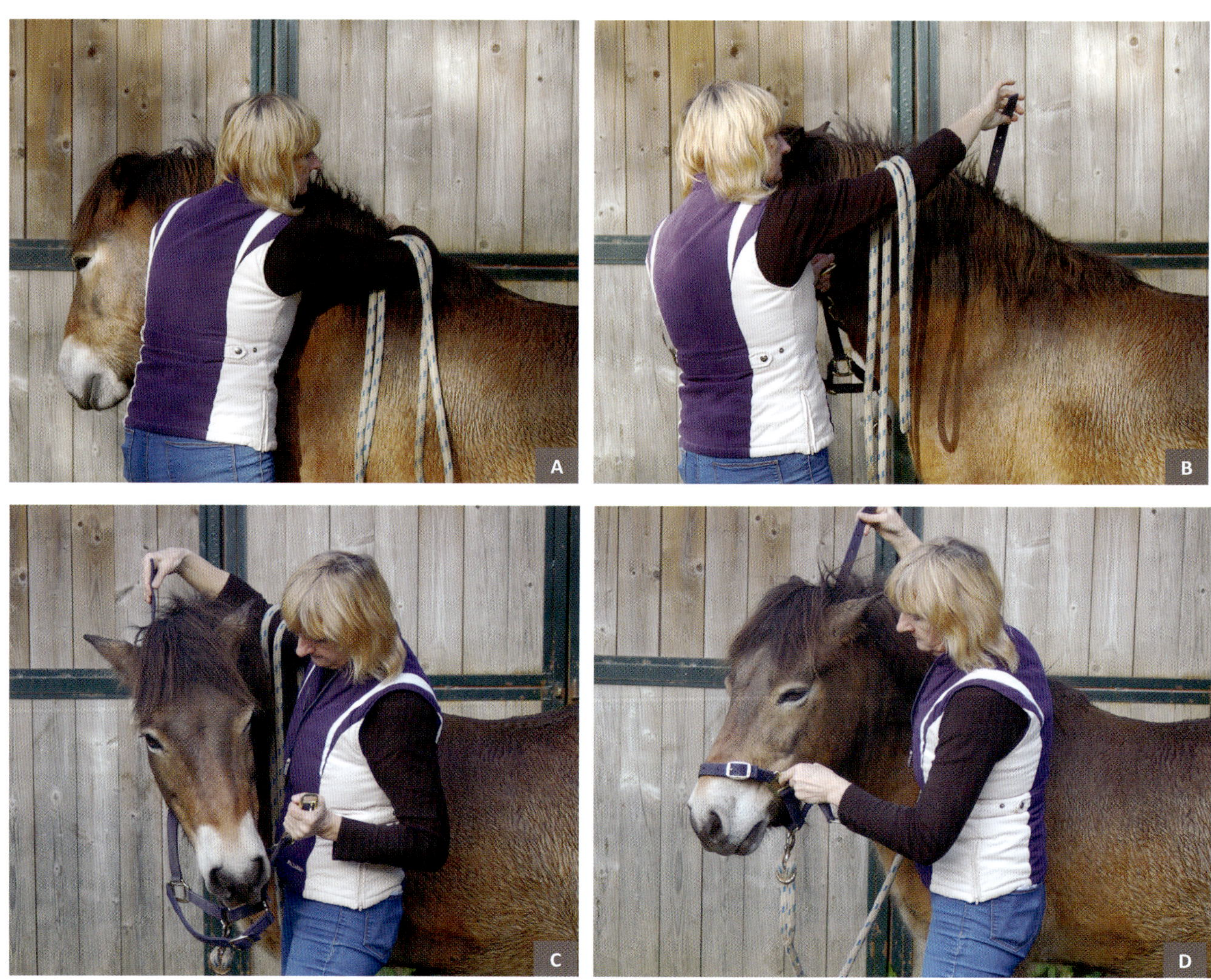

5 A–F I give Ricky a hug with the halter poll strap in my left hand (A). I bring the poll strap up his neck (B), then ask him to bring his nose around to me, using the poll strap to guide him (C). On goes the noseband (D), and I do the halter up (E). Ricky and I are now connected and ready to work together (F).

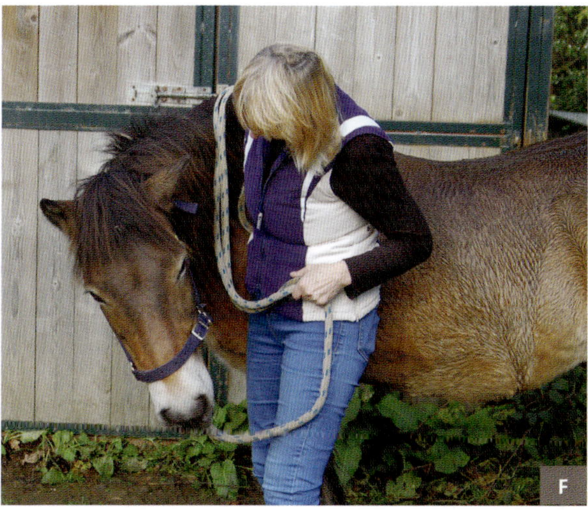

I pass the poll strap to my right hand, then work that poll strap up the neck and ask the horse to bend his nose round to me so I can very carefully ease his nose into the noseband. Then, I can do it up (figs. 5 A–F). It's all very smooth and slow, with no possibility of catching the halter on any sensitive areas. I feel good about it, and I think the horse does, too.

WHAT IF

Remember that when you put a halter on a horse, you become his protector as he can no longer defend himself by running away.

Some horses, due to past ill treatment (deliberate or not) may not be happy to be haltered in this way. You may find your horse prefers you to stand in front or even on the right-hand side. Spend time helping him understand that wearing a halter is a good thing and that putting it on does not need to be scary.

EXERCISE 6
Lowering the Head

WHAT IT IS

You want your horse to feel relaxed before he starts a day with you. Here are a few ideas to help him feel that way.

You will have seen from *Exercise 2: Observing Something New* (p. 19) how your horse reacts when he is afraid, so by now, you'll be able to read his state of mind a lot more clearly and help him relax for the day ahead. A lot of horses become very stiff and tight in their heads and necks when they feel unsure about something. Even if you feel that your horse is absolutely fine and ready to get on with the job, I would like you to try these simple movements with him and see how freely he can move his heads and necks around.

We are going to ask him to drop his head, not for food, but to lower his head using a little feel on the lead rope.

HOW TO DO IT

Stand beside your horse, who should already be wearing a halter and lead rope. Don't stand in front of him because he may throw his head up and catch you in the face.

Reach under his chin and, with your fingertips on the lead rope, ask him to lower his head. It's important that this is a light "ask" with the fingers, because if you go in too strong, he will pull against you (figs. 6 A & B). Even if he only lowers his head a tiny bit, let him know that's a good answer, first by releasing the ask on the rope, then rewarding him using whatever motivates him: food, a scratch, or just leaving him alone (*Exercise 3: What Motivates Your Horse?*, p. 24).

Then, ask again. Each time you ask him, you are looking for the head to go a bit lower and to become easier to move as he relaxes. His neck should be moving up and down, hinged at the withers and the poll, and reaching forward as if he is grazing, not inward toward his chest. It should feel like a well-oiled hinge.

WHAT IF

Sometimes, it just seems impossible to move the horse's head. By observing him when he is loose in his stall or pasture, check that he can lower his head to graze or reach around to scratch himself. If he can do it himself, it

probably isn't pain that is stopping him from lowering his head when you ask.

Make sure your ask is very light and soft. The harder you push and pull, the more he'll want to resist you. Just set up the question and wait for the answer. You don't even need to be looking at him because you'll feel the looseness come before you ever see it. When you do feel that tiny looseness, stop asking immediately and let him know that was a good answer.

A horse that can move his head in this way is not afraid and is ready to start having a conversation with the handler.

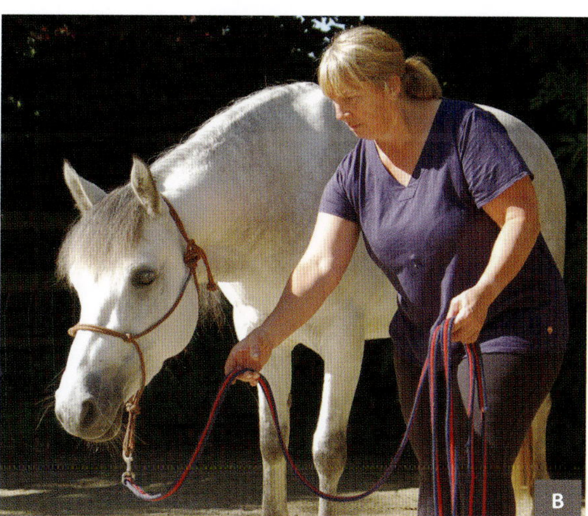

6 A & B Keep your head and face right out of the way as you ask the horse to lower his head (A). See if you can stand upright while the horse keeps his head low (B).

EXERCISE 7

EXERCISE 7
Bending from the Poll to the Withers

WHAT IT IS

You're going to ask the horse to bend his neck by bringing his head around toward you and then away from you so that his neck curves from the poll right through to the withers, while keeping his ears horizontal.

HOW TO DO IT

Stand beside your horse and with the rope, or with your fingertips gently holding onto the noseband, ask him to bring his head round to you (fig. 7 A). You are not just looking for the nose, you want the whole head to come round to you with the ears horizontal so there isn't a twist in the neck. Look for the tiniest attempt by your horse, and let him know that it's all right to try.

7 A & B Ricky brings his head softly around when I ask him (A). His ears are almost horizontal with only a slight twist in the neck. He was very fearful of looking away like this when he first came to live with me because he didn't like losing sight of his handler (B).

When you've got something good happening toward you, even if it's tiny, try asking him to take his head *away* from you so that he's looking over his shoulder the other way. Some horses may find this difficult as they don't want to lose sight of the handler, but look for those little tries and let him know it's okay (fig. 7 B).

All these movements should be loose and smooth with no strength needed from you to achieve them.

WHAT IF

As with the previous exercise (*Exercise 6: Lowering the Head*, p. 34), do not try to pull or push the horse's head. You are asking him to release his poll and for that release to travel down the vertebrae of the neck until it reaches the withers. This is not easy for some horses. Remember, if their head twists, they are avoiding releasing all those vertebrae and there may be something painful going on.

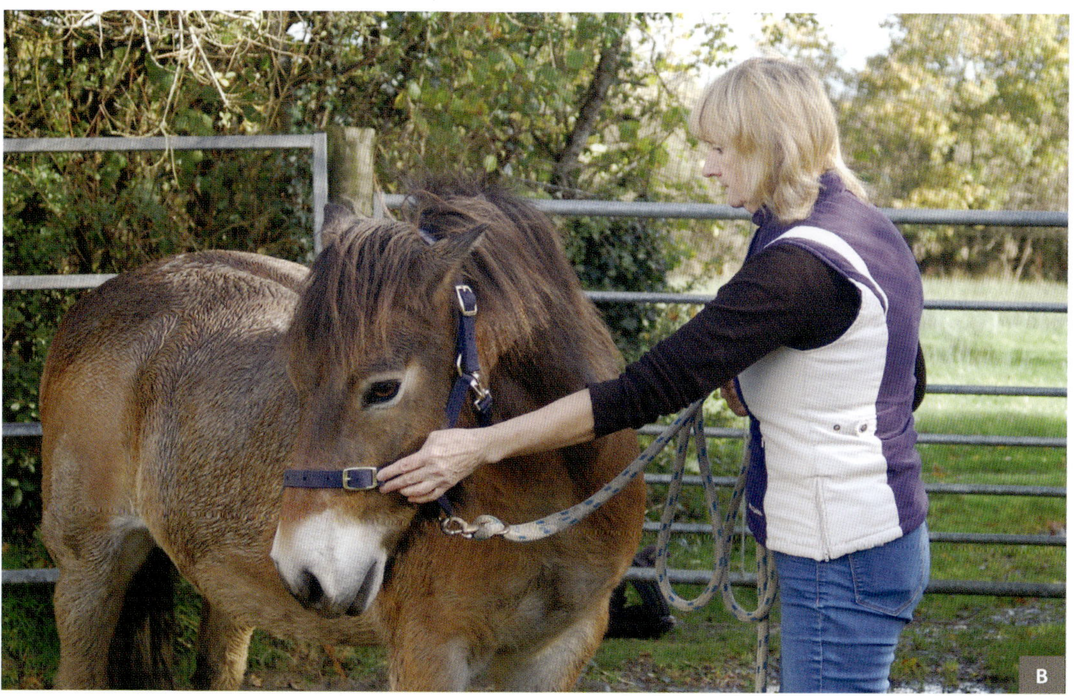

EXERCISE 8
Standing Still

WHAT IT IS

A horse that can stand still and wait for his next instruction means that you, as handler or rider, don't need to be constantly trying to keep him still while you attend to another job. It's also a safety issue because sometimes you really do need him to stand still and wait—at a mounting block or a road crossing, for example. Just being able to relax while you wait to go into the show ring or present yourself to the judge can make a huge difference to your competition nerves.

HOW TO DO IT

Ask your horse to "Wait." This needs to be very clear to him and not confused with any other cue (fig. 8 A). You can use the word

8 A & B Carol asks Libby to stand still and slowly moves away (A). She then asks Libby to come to her while taking a small step back to encourage her to come (B).

"Wait" or use a hand signal—whatever works for you. Still holding the lead rope, step away, count to one, and return to your horse. Be careful not to pull on the rope as that may cause him to walk toward you. Only when you can walk away without the horse trying to walk with you can you go on to the next stage.

You're now going to ask him to come to you after you have walked away (fig. 8 B). The rope will help you here. Have a

signal that is very clear such as the word, "Come" or a hand signal. Step away from the horse, wait a short time (a few seconds to start with), then ask him to walk to you.

Your horse may be a bit confused by this at first because you've been walking away and not allowing him to follow. Give him time to work out that when you give the "Come" signal, it's giving him permission to move toward you. To help him, you can take a step back, almost as if you are

making a space for him to move into (figs. 8 C & D). Put a little tension on the lead rope if you need to, but not a pull. When he steps toward you, be lavish in your praise.

Repeat these steps until you can ask him to "Wait" and you can walk right to the end of the lead rope without him moving, and then ask him to walk to you.

Now let's look at two different sorts of "Wait."

The first "Wait" he must learn is that when the rope or reins are left on the ground, he is "ground-tied," which means he must not move.

In the second sort of "Wait," the rope or reins are off the ground, perhaps over his neck, so if I ask him to walk to me, he is free to do so because the reins are not on the ground.

The "rules" are:

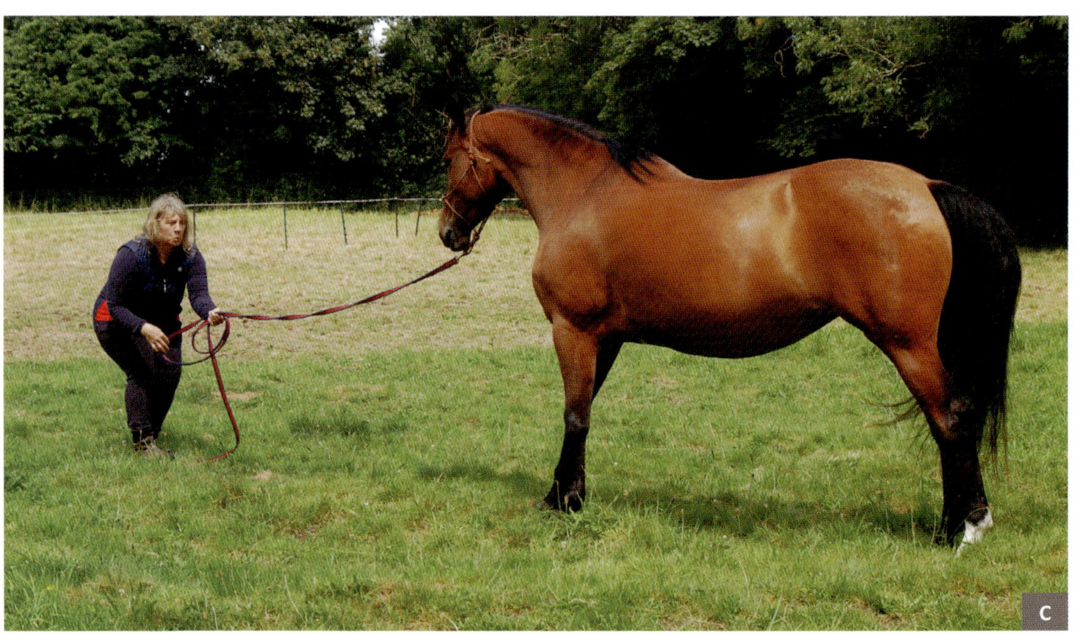

8 C & D Libby is "stuck." She is unsure about walking to Carol (C). It is really important not to pull here. Carol just waits for the horse to make a decision to walk. When she does, Carol doesn't "reel her in" on a tight rope (D). She wants the horse to come on a light feel, not a pull.

1. When the rope is *on* the ground, he must *not move.*

2. When the rope is *off* the ground, he *can move.*

These differences are useful. Suppose I am out for a ride and I fall off. I always trail ride with a long lead rope attached to the halter on my horse, the end of which is tucked into my belt. When I fall off, the rope pulls free and drags on the ground. My horse will stop because he has been taught he must "Wait" when the rope or reins are on the ground.

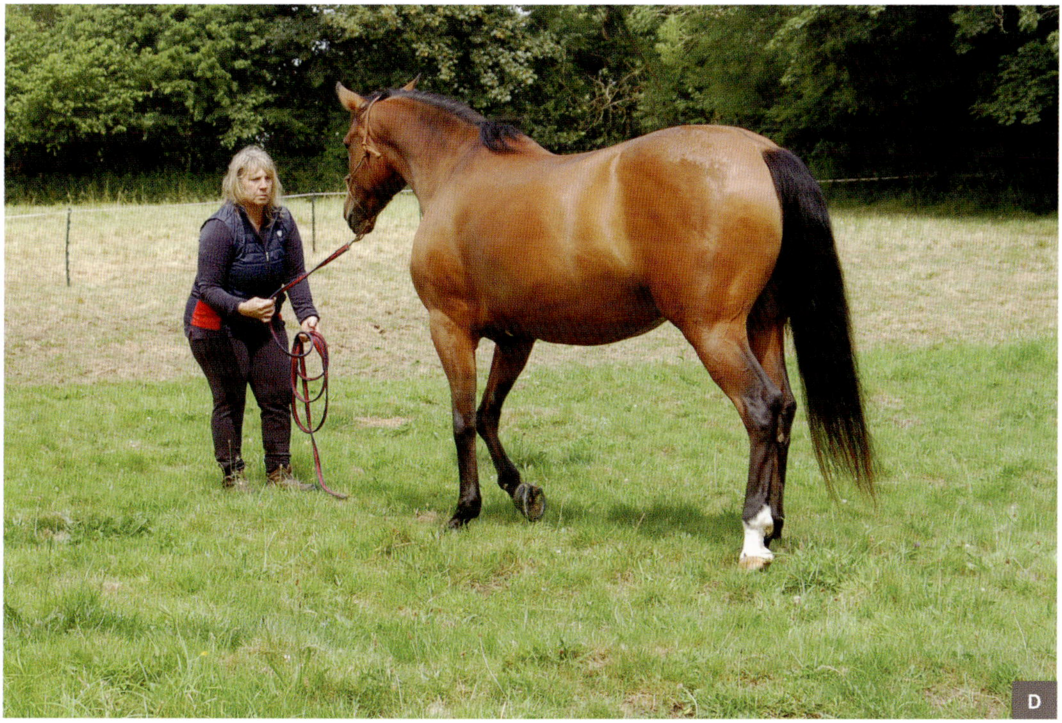

But sometimes I want him to wait, then come to me when I call him. For example, if I'm out for a trail ride, and I need to clear a way through an overgrown path, I might ask him to wait while I move brush out of the way, then ask him to join me.

As long as you are clear in your signals from the start, you'll be surprised how quickly the horse understands the difference between the two "Waits."

Pick a place where the horse is comfortable standing still but can move if he needs to. With a halter and lead rope on the horse, drop the rope in a coil in front of him, and give a very clear signal to wait. This can be a hand signal or just the word "Wait," as you did before when you were still holding on to the lead rope. Then step back, count to one, and return to him. If he hasn't moved, give him a rub, or whatever works for him, to let him know that was the right answer.

Next, ask for "Wait," but step a bit farther away and count to one. You are slowly increasing the distance but not the time away from him. You can extend the wait time later; just get him to understand that he doesn't need to join you as you walk away. Your aim is to be able to ask him to wait with the rope on the ground, and without him moving, while you move all round him.

(See *What If* for what to do if he moves.)

Now, you are going to look at doing exactly the same thing, but without the lead rope on the ground. I call this "parking" my horse. When I've parked him, I want to know he'll be there when I go back for him. Follow the same instructions as for ground-tying him. When he can stand without feeling he has to move, you can start to ask him to come to you.

WHAT IF

When your horse keeps moving in the "Wait," keep the distance you step away really small and ensure the signal to "Wait" is very clear so he's in no doubt that is what you need him to do. If he moves, do not reassure or stroke him, simply put him back in the exact place you asked him to "Wait," repeat the signal, and move away again. Don't hammer away at this. You're looking for tiny moments of understanding. (In my previous book *3-Minute Horsemanship,* I discuss these moments in much greater detail.)

EXERCISE 9
Easy Leading

WHAT IT IS

Once you've haltered your horse, you want him to follow your lead in a relaxed way. A horse that leads on a loose lead rope without pulling or barging into the handler is a joy to take out and about (figs. 9 A & B). Whatever happens, you know that you can safely take that horse anywhere without worrying he doesn't know how to stay with the handler.

I can honestly say I didn't learn how to lead a horse until well into my middle age. All we did as children was go into the field, put a halter on our ponies, and drag them in behind us. Along the way we battled to stop them from heading for the grassy lawn or stepping on our feet, and if we reached the stable without going to all four points of the compass we'd done pretty well.

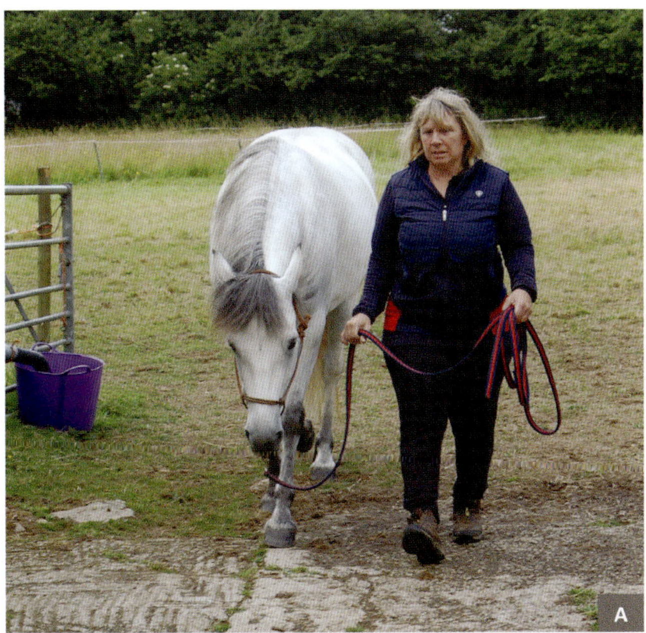

9 A & B A horse like Melody is easy to lead and is a joy for Carol to handle (A). Don't let your lead rope become too long, as shown here, or the horse can tread on it (B).

HOW TO DO IT

I have seen people trying to lead their horses by grasping the lead rope clip under the chin and dragging the animal along as if their life depended on it. Some do get where they want to go, but why make it such hard work (fig. 9 C)? Teaching the horse to follow the feel of the lead rope instead of a pull is easy—just don't pull.

Teaching a horse to "lead on a feel" means leading him with a loose rope. If you find someone who's willing to take the role of the horse and ask her to hold on to the end of the lead rope, you can play around with the rope and see how little you need to do for the "horse" to feel the rope moving. When each movement of the rope means something to the horse, and he is trained to understand what these movements of the rope mean, you don't need to pull at all.

9 C When you hang on a horse, it makes leading very hard work.

Horses move in four different directions: forward, backward, left, and right (and upward, but we won't go into that here!) so you will need four different ways of handling the rope to achieve each of these. When the horse is being led, this should feel easy and loose, as if he's on roller skates.

Decide what your signal is to get your horse moving. Is it a vocal cue, "Walk on," or a hand signal? It really doesn't matter as long as it's the same signal every time.

Often when I'm teaching, I ask people to walk their horse forward. So much begins to happen then that I'm surprised the horse can sort out all the signals and find the right answer. People click their tongues, say "Walk on," pull on the rope, shuffle their feet forward—and these are just what I can see and hear. The horse is seeing a whole lot more, I'm sure.

I then ask handlers what their cue is to ask the horse to walk. They always give me one answer and when I point out they did many different things, they are amazed because they just didn't realize how much they were doing. We then work through all those different signals, and by using each one in isolation, quickly find the ones that

THE MOST IMPORTANT GAIT

Of course, the most important gait to master is the stop. The stop is non-negotiable for me. When I need a horse to stop, I need it *right now*, not halfway across the road or in some other potentially dangerous situation. Get good at stopping your horse on the lead. It could save both your lives.

don't work and the one that does. We want our communication with the horse to be clear and simple; he shouldn't need to second-guess you all the time.

Once you've got the cue sorted, you can decide on your leading position. You can walk in front or beside or right behind. These are all correct leading positions and have their uses somewhere in handling horses. My feeling is that you need to get comfortable with your horse in all these leading positions, so they are available if you need them in different situations.

Why not try leading from the right-hand side of the horse? Traditionally, we always lead on the left, but this goes back to soldiers and where they carried their swords, so unless you're planning to be so armed, you can dispense with that idea and lead from either side. Your horse may find this a bit disconcerting to start with and keep trying to get you to swap sides because he's not used to you being there. Be quietly persistent, and reassure him that it's fine. You'll find it odd too, perhaps, but after a while you'll probably forget which side you are "supposed" to lead on.

WHAT IF

Let's say you can't get your horse moving other than by pulling on his head. This is very common, so don't worry. To get a horse to walk forward without pulling just means you need to create some energy that encourages him to move in the direction you desire. Here's the way I do it: I raise the hand that is holding the rope and point as if I'm showing the way I want the horse to go. I'm not putting any tension on the rope at all; it is still loose. I then add my "Walk on" cue, which is me raising my energy, looking forward with focus, and preparing my body

to take that step. I don't actually step, but I look as though I'm just about to. I want my horse to take that initial step and then I will step with him so that we move forward together.

At first, the horse might not understand, so I might tap him on his body where my leg would be if I were riding him. I don't get hard; I just keep tapping lightly. It's not a hitting motion, which is important to know. You don't need to get heavy with a horse to make him move. You can learn that from a tiny fly, who can get a whole herd of horses moving up into the gallop just by annoying them!

The moment your horse answers your request for him to move forward (and it may be a tiny little try to start with), stop asking, lower your hand (if using it) and energy, and praise him. I repeat this until I consistently get a step forward when I ask. I then look for two steps, then more, until the horse understands that when I raise my hand to show him which way to go and indicate my intention to walk forward, he should take that first step.

EXERCISE 10
Backing Up

WHAT IT IS

A horse that backs up willingly and with lightness can be moved in and out of tight areas that he cannot turn around in.

Nearly 60 years ago, when I was first learning to ride, a pony taught me how to back him up. I was being a brat (well, I was about five years old), and I was blaming my pony for everything that was going wrong in my lesson. Eventually, the pony had had enough, so much so that he ran off with me back toward his stall. Unfortunately for him, the gate was closed, so there we were in a narrow entrance to the barn, with nowhere to go. I had no idea how to get out of this jam; there was absolutely no room to turn. Being five years old, I started to cry, but interestingly, I *did* know why the pony had run off with me. I knew I had been behaving badly toward him.

I heard a noise behind me and there was my instructor. "Well, you deserved that," she stated calmly. "Now you'd better work out how to go backward, and if I were you, I'd ask the pony."

It was that word "ask" that stuck with me. Not "tell," but "ask."

I sat there and thought about it, and after a while I realized that we couldn't go forward so I would have to ride backward. I have to confess, for a fleeting moment I did nearly turn around in the saddle and face the other way, but I figured out that wasn't going to help because the pony's head would be in the wrong place!

Time passed in which I tried a few things that didn't work. Then I realized that if I stopped the pony from going forward by using my reins, but still rode him as if we were going forward, he might get the idea that I wanted him to move somewhere other than ahead. I think the closed gate helped us a bit, too, but sooner or later, I had ridden the pony backward out of that narrow gap.

I still back up my horses on the ground and in the saddle using the same technique, today. I "close the space in front," as it were, but keep the intention to move, so the only direction open to move into is backward.

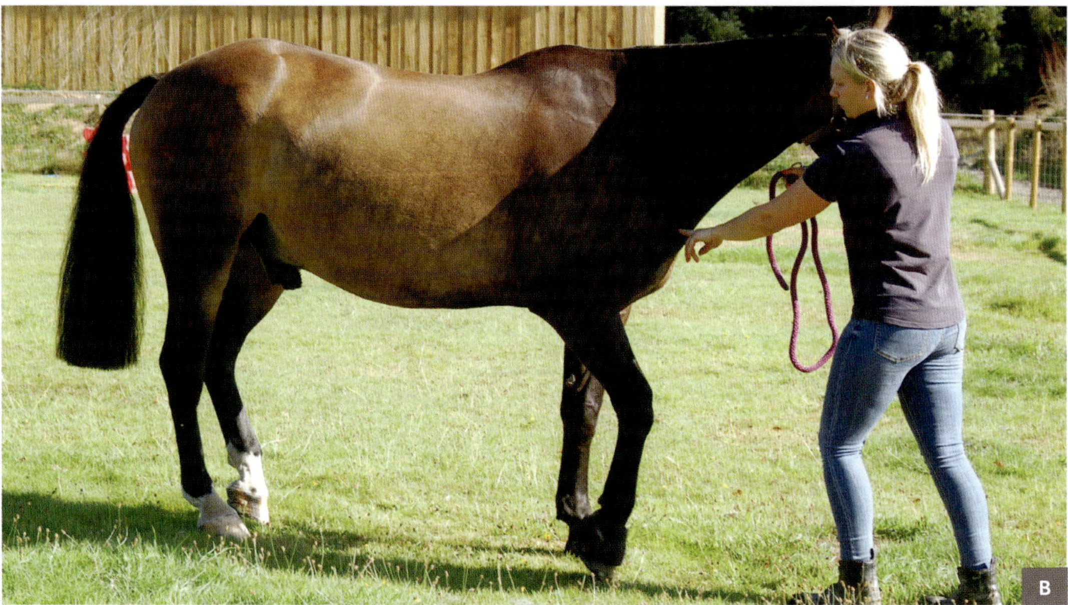

10 A & B There are lots of different ways to back up your horse. One is tapping the lead rope and creating a little vibration on the noseband of the halter (A). Becky puts a little pressure on Archie's chest to ask him to step away (B).

HOW TO DO IT

Just like when asking horse to walk forward, there are a number of ways to ask him to go backward. The principle is exactly the same: your energy is up, you've just closed the "front door" and left the "back door" open.

To ask a horse to back up from the ground, you can press on his nose or chest, or you can grasp the lead rope clip under his chin and push back toward his chest. These are great starting points, but it's really useful to teach a cue that doesn't require being close to the horse, such as a vocal cue or a hand signal—but not both. Remember, you are trying to simplify things here.

To train a new signal, I suggest you use the new signal immediately followed by signal you used previously so that the horse begins to connect the two. In Photo 10 A, you can see Carol asking Melody to back up by tapping the rope. She taught her horse to do this by first pressing on Melody's chest and putting in the vocal cue, "Back up," to ask the horse to back away (fig. 10 B). Very soon Carol could just use the words, so she began to experiment with other ways, such as tapping the rope with a finger while using the same vocal cue. Soon Melody did not need the words; the lightest finger tap on the rope would cause her to back away. One day Carol didn't have a lead rope on her horse, so she *pretended* to tap on a lead rope, and to her amazement, Melody backed up. The *movement* of the tapping finger had become the cue. This doesn't take long. Horses are pretty clever and they will quickly connect signals and begin to react to the remote signal.

WHAT IF

What happens if your horse doesn't back up and pushes his front feet into the ground, deciding he's just not going backward for anyone? Remember the five reasons why a horse won't do what you want (see p. 26)? Pain is often a thing to look out for here: to go backward, the horse has to raise his back and engage his hindquarters, and for some, this can be painful. Also, make sure that he's not afraid because you are asking him to back up into something, such as a wall or fence.

When I have a horse that I know is not afraid or in pain but just doesn't understand, I use a "method" that I picked up from Buck Brannaman, an American horseman from whom I have learned a great deal. His goal is to make the horse feel safe

10 C I learned a specific hand position to help a horse back up from horseman Buck Brannaman.

and secure around humans by working with the horse's nature and understanding how he thinks. I grasp the lead rope clip under the horse's chin with my elbow up and my thumb pointing down toward the ground, and gently rock the horse's head from side to side over his shoulders until I feel the slightest softening backward; then I stop and praise (fig. 10 C). I just keep quietly and calmly doing this until we get a step back. This may be all I achieve that day, but in a very short time, the horse will have the confidence to step backward, and I can then start to train in a "remote" cue.

Showery

EXERCISE 11
Dancing Together

WHAT IT IS

Have you ever seen two horses that don't really know each other turned out in adjoining paddocks? Did you notice how they moved up and down the fenceline, mirroring each other's movements? They turn, they trot, they even swing their heads at times, as if they are performing some intricate dance.

This is called *synchronization*, and there is a theory that when horses first meet, they practice this dance so that when they have to run away from danger, they don't run into each other.

If you watch a pair of driving horses, they'll often be moving along using the same sequence of movement in the feet, and closely bonded horses grazing together in a field often move in the same way, stepping forward with the same foot as they move along.

HOW TO DO IT

Playing around with this idea is a really fun thing to do on a rainy day. You can do this on a lead rope or with your horse loose in a safe area.

Lead the horse in walk, and when he's walking forward in a nice even rhythm, start to copy him. Match up to his front legs with your legs, allowing him to set the pace; just copy him until you are totally in harmony with him.

Then start to change the way you walk.

You can walk very slowly or very fast; you can take giant steps or tiny steps. Watch the horse begin to copy your way of moving. When he seems to be getting the idea that you are both synchronized, you can start to change the way you walk more dramatically. You could try backing up and to the side, moving in time with horse's feet (figs. 11 A–C).

Experiment and have fun. It's not a competition (figs. 11 D & E). When you feel ready, you can try lifting one knee very high, pointing out your toe, and then

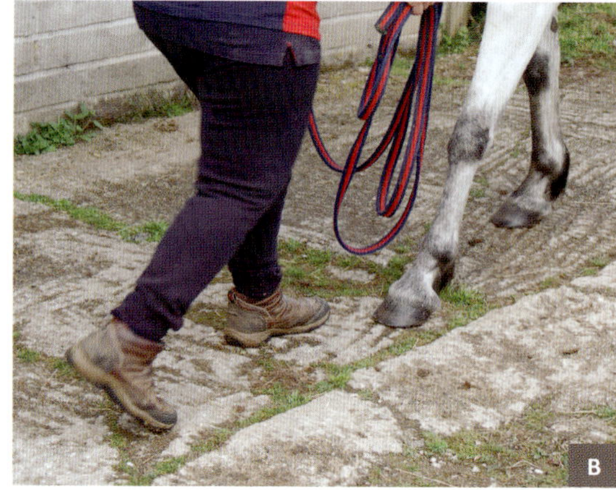

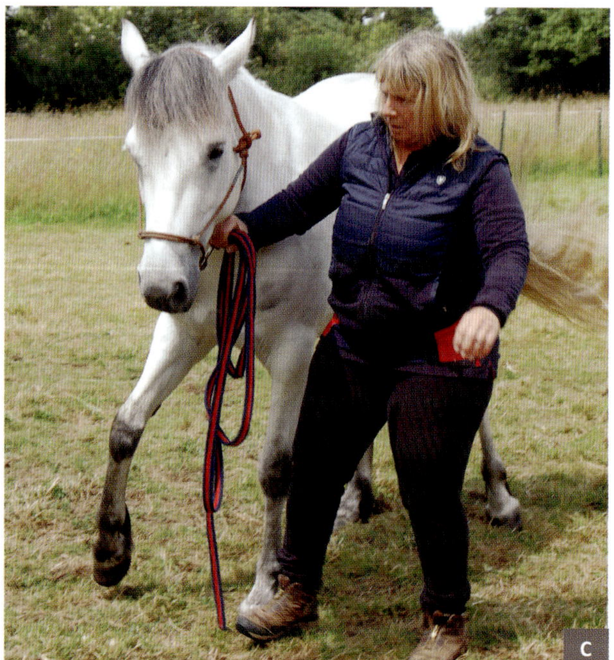

11 A–E Carol is getting in time with Melody's feet as she backs away (A & B). They begin the "dance" (C). Daisy and Lesley moving together, perfectly synchronized (D & E).

putting down your foot. Then repeat this with the other leg. When you are synchronized with your horse, you'll find he starts to look down at your legs and will try to copy you, almost in Spanish Walk!

WHAT IF

Sometimes, a horse doesn't understand what you are doing. Let him look down at your legs, and don't go too fast. He needs to be able to read the pattern and copy you.

At the beginning, make sure you synchronize with him first, then very slowly change your footfall and give him time to realize what you are doing. This is real horse communication—you aren't speaking human, you're speaking horse.

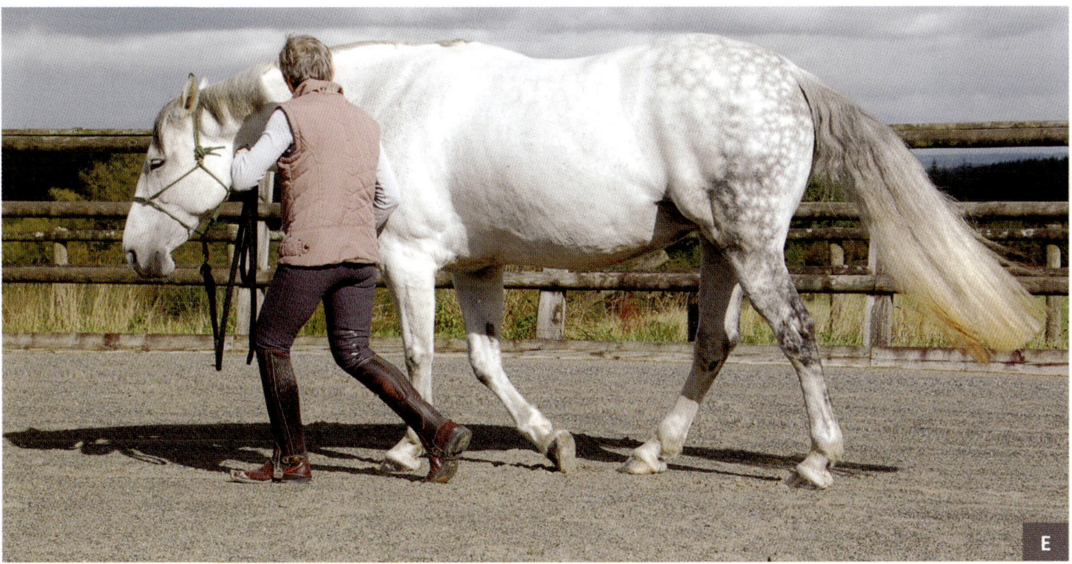

Moving the Hind End Around

move his hind end over to fit sideways into a compartment. Knowing how to move the back end independently of the front end can be very useful.

WHAT IT IS

Just as it's important to be able to move the horse backward and forward, it's equally important to be able to move each end of him so you can change direction. Opening and closing a gate on horseback is all about moving the front and back ends of the horse, and when loading into some horse trailers, the horse is required to walk in and

HOW TO DO IT

To be able to do this, the horse has to get his body into a particular shape so that his legs are able to easily move to take the correct steps. If he is going to step to the right with his hind end, he swings his rib cage to the right. That gives him room for the left hind foot to step underneath his body. He may need to step away with his right foot first to

A

B

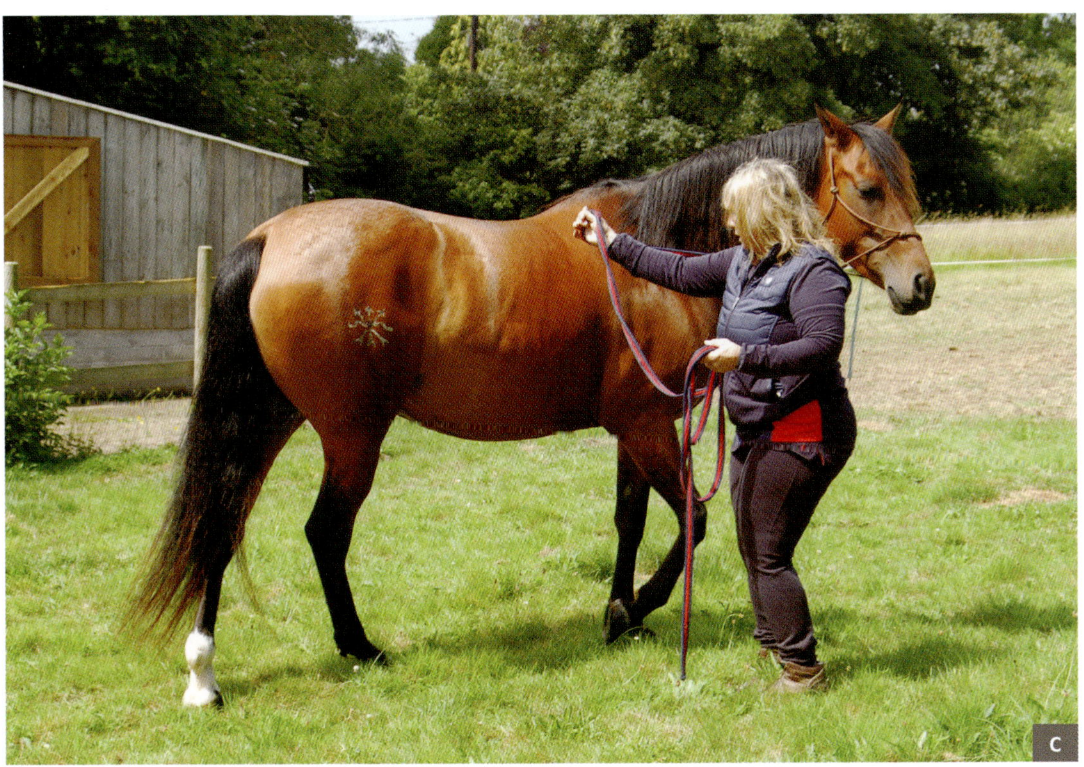

12 A–C The rope here is a little tight in Photo A, and Daisy is anticipating Lesley's hand on her hip, so she's moving before the hand touches her. The pair is better in Photo B. The rope is much softer. Carol does not need to touch Libby to ask her to move over in Photo C. The use of the rope is enough of a signal to get the hindquarters to yield.

make room for that left foot, but it's the ribs I want you to be aware of.

If you look over your left shoulder, you will feel your ribs move to the right. Even on two legs, looking over your left shoulder like this will make it easier for you to step to the right. Try it!

With a halter and rope on your horse for safety, rest your hand on his hindquarters (figs. 12 A & B). Lift the rope a little to bring his head around to you. It doesn't need to be all the way round. (In the photos you can see Daisy's head is not very far around toward Lesley, but it is enough to help those ribs move away.) Raise your energy as if you are about to walk into him and put a little pressure onto his hindquarters. You will probably feel him move a little. Let him know that's the right answer, then ask again. Soon he'll get the idea and step away. Do not use slaps or loud noises to move him; just ask him to step away from you.

WHAT IF

When the horse does the opposite of what you want and pushes into you, lift the hand that is holding the lead rope a little higher, about level with his cheek. Don't pull, just lift, and this will cause his head to come round to you a little more, almost as if he looking over his shoulder. Put your hand on his hindquarters and raise your energy as if you are going to walk into him, and wait, and wait, and wait. So many people give up too soon. Just WAIT. The horse has got to work out what he has to do to straighten out his body. He won't want to be bent like this for long. He might pull on you, but don't pull back; just hold and wait. After a short time (always less than three minutes), the horse will soften and move away. It may only be a hair's breadth but it's a start. Don't get in a battle here—ask and wait.

Eventually, you won't need to touch the horse to get him to step over, you will simply use the lead rope to get him into a good shape to step away as you lift the rope (fig. 12. C).

EXERCISE 13
Moving the Front End Around

WHAT IT IS

Here, you are asking the horse to keep his hind end as still as he can and move his front end around it. As I explained in *Exercise 12: Moving the Hind End Around* (p. 54), being able to move your horse in all directions is so important because you want to be able to get in and out of tight spaces. If you can only go forward or backward, how are you going to ride around a corner?

When you go around a very sharp bend, such as a small circle, the horse has to use both his back and his front end to make that turn so he doesn't fall over. At some point, you've probably heard someone say a horse "drops his shoulder" on a turn. This is because he's not stepping out with that shoulder to stay upright and balanced.

HOW TO DO IT

With a halter and lead rope on your horse, stand beside his head. Look back at how you asked the horse to move his head away from you in *Exercise 7* (p. 36): you asked the horse to look away from you by using your fingertips softly. You weren't pushing, you were *asking*.

Now, you want that "ask" to have a bit

13 A The hand position on the halter and on the shoulder.

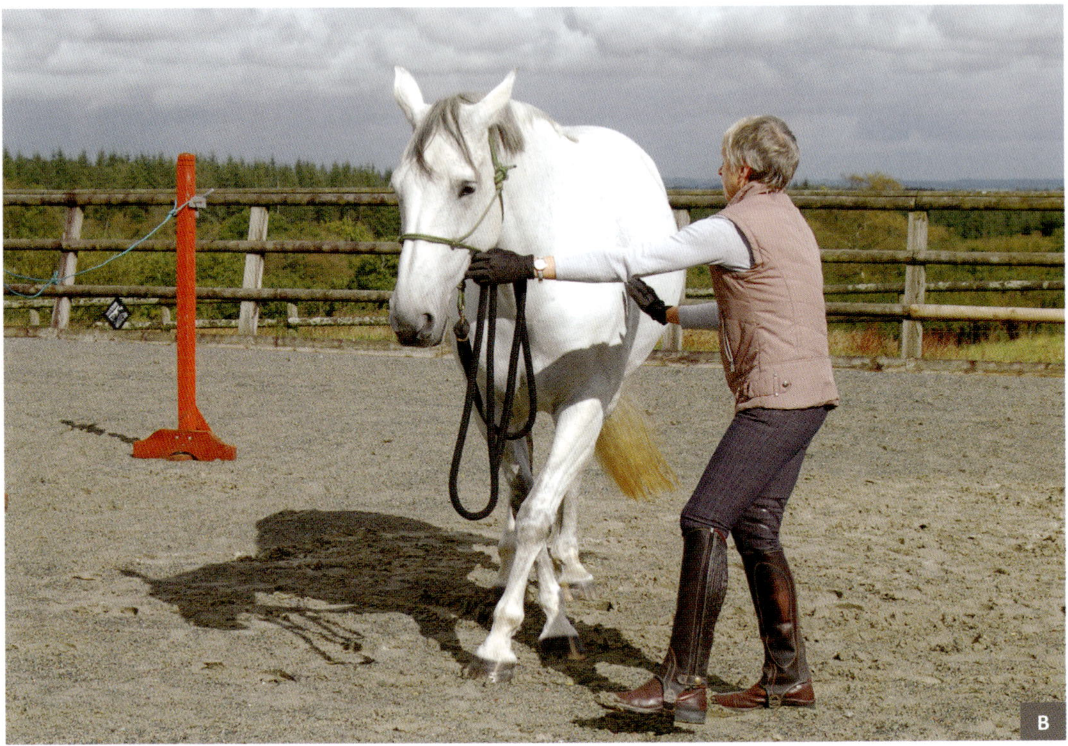

13 B A nice step over with the left front foot by Daisy.

more energy in it, as if you are going to walk into his head. At first, all he'll do is look away, but keep your energy up, because now you want him to start to move his feet (fig. 13 A). As most horses are naturally on their forehand, a lot of their weight is on the front feet, so most will find this quite difficult at first. When they are perfectly balanced, they are prepared to take a nice easy step over (fig. 13 B).

WHAT IF

What do you do if your horse will not step over? It's usually because he's got all his weight forward and he just can't pick up those front feet. Try asking him to rock his weight back to take some of the load off the front feet. It doesn't matter what foot he moves first or whether he crosses his legs over. All you're looking for is for him to easily step those front feet over.

Moving the Feet

WHAT IT IS

If you could move each of your horse's feet to exactly the place you want, wouldn't that make life a lot easier? Think about the act of loading your horse into a trailer. Wouldn't it be so simple?

There is a lot going on when you try to load a horse, especially when a horse has a bad association with trailers. For most of us, we're trying not to get run over, to get the horse to stay straight, to keep him looking into the loading space, to stop pulling and pushing. It's overwhelming.

HOW TO DO IT

So, let's stop and break the whole thing down into separate tasks, and just load one foot at a time. Forget the horse—move his *feet,* because where his feet go, the horse must follow. If you can choose a foot and move it forward, then choose the next foot in the sequence and move that one, eventually all four feet—and, of course, the horse—will be in the trailer.

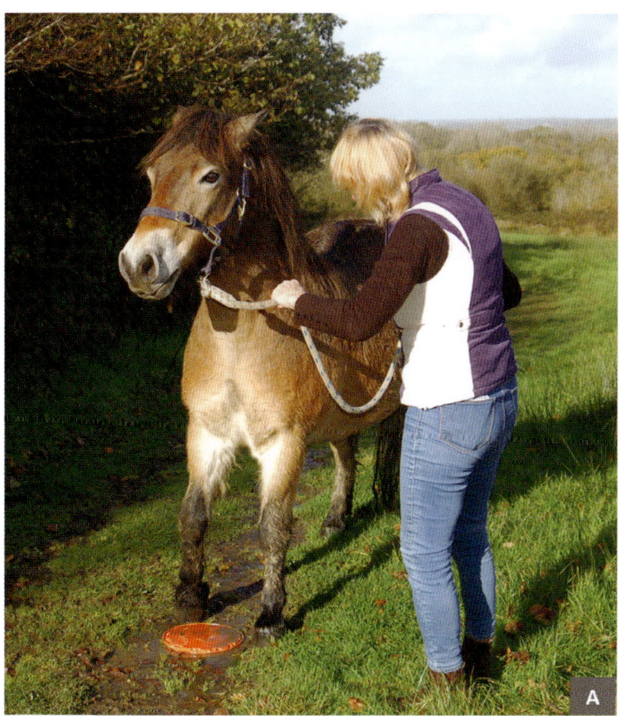

14 A Timing is everything here. As the horse's foot is lifting, I am directing it to step onto the plastic marker.

In days past, we used to do this with our ponies by lifting each foot by hand and stepping it forward, and strangely it did work, but here's an easier way.

Think of the sequence of a horse's feet as he walks forward. It can start with the right hind; the right front steps forward out of the way, the left hind steps forward, and the left front moves out of the way. And so the sequence repeats itself. Because of the

14 B Then I give Ricky a rest before asking anything more, because that works well for him.

way your horse is standing, he might not start at the beginning of that sequence, but wherever he starts is how his feet move, one after the other. The walk has a four-time beat when you listen to it.

Using a target (like a bucket lid or just a mark on the ground), choose a foot on your horse and move him around until your chosen foot is stepping on the target (fig. 14 A). You don't physically bend down to hold that foot and put it on the mark. Instead, you lead the horse very specifically to move

his feet onto that mark. You have the skills to stop him (*Exercise 8: Standing Still,* p. 38), lead him forward (*Exercise 9: Easy Leading,* p. 43), to back him up (*Exercise 10: Backing Up,* p. 47) and move his hind end and forehand around (*Exercises 12* and *13: Moving the Hind End Around* and *Moving the Front End Around,* pp. 54 and 57), you're just putting them into action now to perform a task. Remember to stop asking as soon as he puts his foot onto the marker (fig. 14 B).

Now choose another foot and try again. Pretty soon you can choose any foot and place it anywhere you want.

WHAT IF

Sometimes it's like the horse knows exactly where that mark is and deliberately avoids stepping onto it. Be patient. You just need more time. Remember to look for little triumphs and reward your horse for trying. When you get good at moving his feet, he will go anywhere with you.

EXERCISE 15
Stepping Through Poles

WHAT IT IS

Helping a horse to lift his feet up and step over things without banging his legs protects him from hurting himself. For this exercise, you may want to put protective boots on your horse at first, but once you can get the horse to lift his feet higher, you shouldn't need them (fig. 15). You can use branches or poles. When I use poles, I like to use something like sandbags to stop the poles from rolling, or you can use half-round poles.

Every horse is careful of his legs—it's part of his survival strategy. Some horses panic if they feel something touching their

15 Carol uses a long lead rope so that Melody can pick her way safely through the poles.

legs, so exercises for these stepping up, over, and through need to be done with sensitivity.

HOW TO DO IT

With one pole placed on the ground, ask your horse to walk over it. He might touch it; if he does, see what his reaction is. That will help you plan how soon you can add another pole. You don't want him to jump, just step calmly and quietly over the object. When he's comfortable with one pole, add another, but keep them some distance apart to start with to give him time to think about where he needs to put his feet.

As your horse becomes more confident, you can add more poles and put them closer together. You can also start to change the angles so that they are not parallel to each other. Keep leading your horse over the poles as you add more, and it becomes much more of a pile.

You're looking for calm, confident walking, so do allow your horse to put his head down and pick his way (keep the rope out of the way so he doesn't tread on it or put his foot over it and get tangled). Don't worry if he hits the poles with his feet; you're just giving him confidence so he can move through a "jumble" and remain safe.

WHAT IF

But suppose your horse cannot walk over a pole or branch on the ground? I suggest making the pole really small at first—maybe a lead rope stretched out in a straight line could be a start. Slowly increase the size of the pole. Remember, with all these exercises, you're not in a competition; you're trying to learn more about your horse and how you can help him be more sure of himself in the great big world.

EXERCISE 16
Squeezing Through a Narrow Gap

WHAT IT IS

One of the more dangerous things I see people doing with their horses is walking beside them through narrow spaces. It doesn't take much to squash a human; we're pretty soft compared to a horse in a hurry. In this exercise, you're going to look at how to lead the horse safely through a narrow gap.

HOW TO DO IT

Create a narrow gap with barrels, or use a doorway or space between a wall and a solid object. Ask the horse to "Wait" (see *Exercise 8: Standing Still*—p. 38), walk through the gap yourself, stand to one side, then ask the horse to walk through (figs. 16 A–D). It sounds simple and it is simple,

but I see so many people loading horses into trailers or walking through narrow corridors with the horse beside them. It makes me shiver!

WHAT IF

What should you do if your horse either rushes through the narrow gap or refuses to go through at all? Some horses don't like

16 A Ask your horse to "Wait".

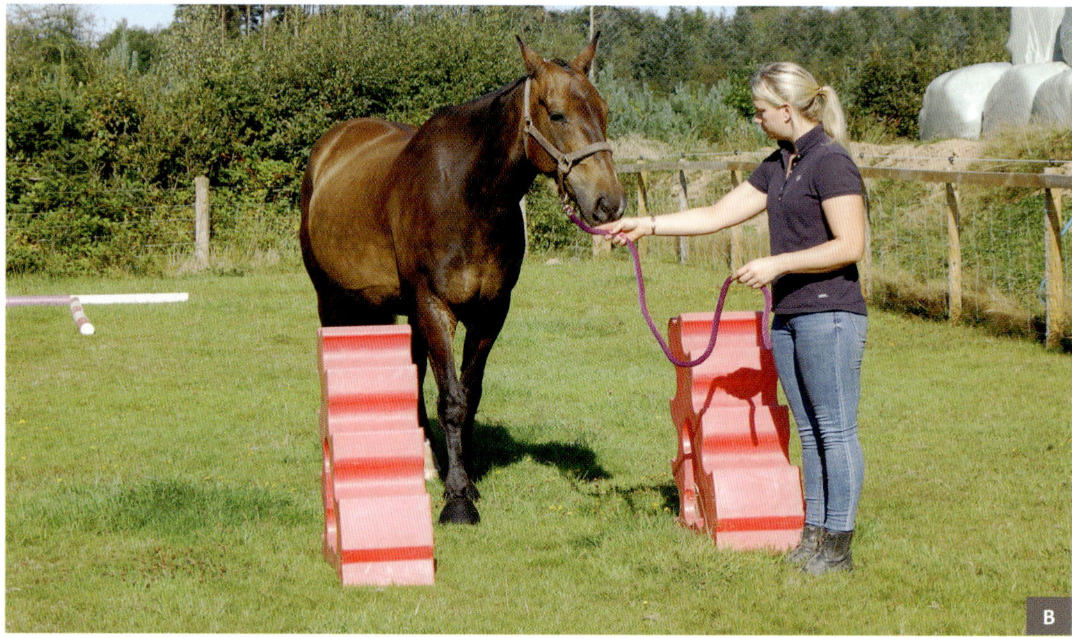

16 B–D Then you walk through the gap to a point where you are safely out of the way (B). Ask the horse to join you (C). This is the safest way to lead a horse through a narrow gateway (D).

the feeling of being trapped as they walk through a narrow space—a very natural fear.

To start with, all you need is make the gap you are passing through very wide. It might need to be as wide as a gateway—maybe wider. Lead him through, following the safe method I've just described until he's happily walking through after you with no concerns.

Then make the gap slightly narrower. This is where big plastic barrels come in handy because they have no sharp edges for the horse to catch himself on, and in a real panic situation, they just fall over. Keep making the gap narrower. If you go too fast and the horse loses his confidence and starts rushing through again, go back and make the gap wider until he's comfortable, then give him a rest before you start again. These rests are so important for a horse who's had a fright, so let him get his adrenaline down before you try again, or better still, after one nice quiet walk through the wider gap, just stop for the day.

EXERCISE 17

Going Under Something Low

WHAT IT IS

In one of my previous books, *Over, Under, Through: Obstacle Training for Horses,* I explored the different aspects of the world that horses find challenging. They can be worried about going *over* something, like a pole on the ground, going *under* a low roof, or squeezing *through* narrow spaces. Growing up with horses, I'd always been told that horses weren't frightened of things over their heads because they didn't have built-in fear of predators coming from above them. But I've found that many horses don't like going under a door frame into their stall or into a trailer with a low

17 A & B In this old barn, Carol has had to teach Libby to lower her head to go under the low door frame.

roof, so perhaps the instinct to fear predators from above is there after all! Your horse may have this fear; you'll know because when you go under low trees or through a gateway with an arch over it, he will raise his head and look up, almost as if he is trying to work out if he might hit his head (figs. 17 A & B).

When you want to train your horse to go under very low obstacles, first of all, I suggest you help him learn to lower his head when you ask him to. You've already looked at that skill in *Exercise 6: Lowering the Head* (p. 34). Once he gets really confident in lowering his head when you ask him, then you can start to introduce safe

17 C & D To practice, I use strips cut from a plastic feed sack to create a low doorway that will not hurt the horse should he raise his head under it (C). As the horse becomes more confident, I can make the strips longer (D).

overhead "obstacles" that he can practice passing beneath.

HOW TO DO IT

A simple way to get started is to use a door frame that already exists or build a simple frame out of water pipe and hang strips of soft material from it (fig. 17 C). This creates a low-hanging "obstacle" without the danger of the horse hurting himself should he raise his head (all he will touch will be soft strips of material). As he becomes more confident, you can make the strips of material longer (fig. 17 D). The solid pipe or door frame needs to be high enough above the horse's head so he cannot bang himself on it as he walks through. Lead him back and forth (see *Exercise 16: Squeezing Through a Narrow Gap*—p. 63) until he finds it easy.

Now start to help him lower his head as he goes through the frame. Halt him so that his head is positioned under the frame, and there, ask him to lower his head. Be gentle here. He needs to feel comfortable about doing this in a place he may find a bit frightening.

Once he can do this, repeat the process, lowering the strips of fabric until they are almost touching his ears. Each time you build his confidence by leading him through, halting him, and asking him to lower his head.

WHAT IF

If your horse absolutely refuses to walk through the frame with even the shortest fabric strips, remove the strips, get him good at walking through without them, add one very short strip and lead him through, then add another, and so on, until he can walk through with confidence.

I hope you can see in this exercise how much you need to break things down into tiny achievable tasks so you don't frighten a horse to the point where he feels he needs to leave a lesson.

EXERCISE 18
Getting a Nice Soft Backup

WHAT IT IS

As we've discussed before, a horse needs to go backward as easily as he can go forward. Just think: if you had a vehicle that couldn't reverse, how inconvenient would that be?

Let's work on getting a really good backup, not just "going backward."

A backup is a soft, smooth movement where the horse's feet move in diagonal pairs. The right front and left hind step back together, then left front and right hind step together (figs. 18 A & B). The secret to a good backup is to make sure you are asking the correct diagonal to move first—in other words, the one that is the next to move

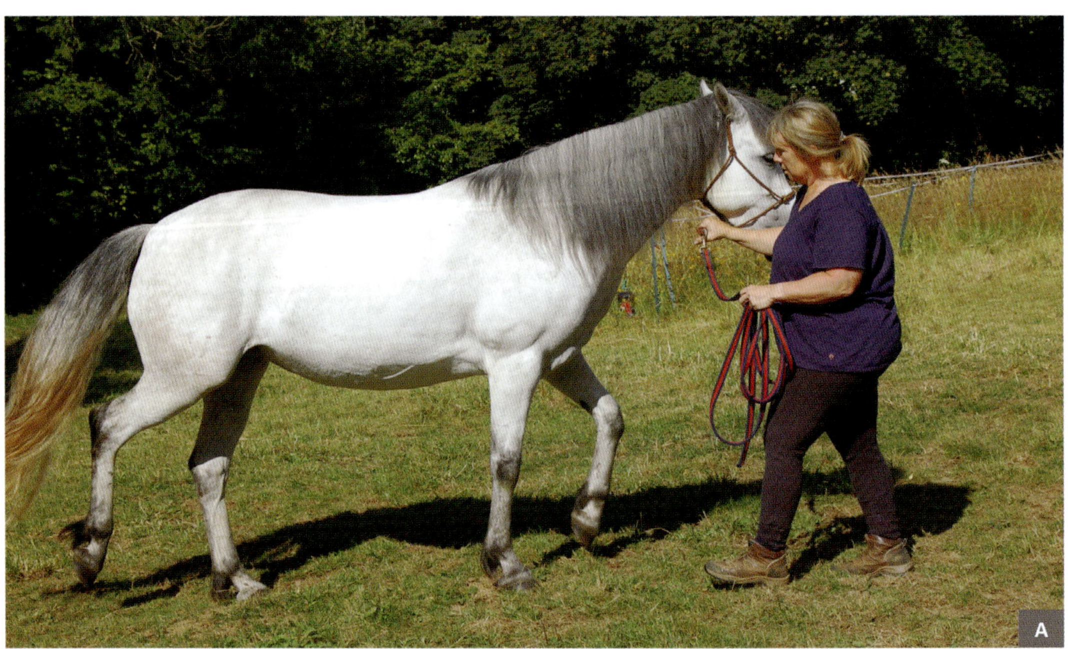

18 A & B In Photo A the left diagonal is stepping back—that's the left front and the right hind moving together backward. In Photo B, you can see that the horse is moving the right hind before the opposite diagonal is ready to move. This will not feel soft to the handler.

in the sequence of footfalls. I have always found that if you get the diagonals swinging through rhythmically, softness just comes as part of the movement.

HOW TO DO IT

If I asked you to stand with your right foot forward and your left foot back, then asked you to step backward, which foot would you choose? It would be the right foot, because that's the easiest. I don't think we really consider this enough when asking a horse to move: asking the *next* foot in the sequence of footfalls to move first.

Look back at *Exercise 10: Backing Up* (p. 47) to see various ways in which you can back up your horse. Before you ask your horse to go backward, look at how his feet are arranged on the ground. The front foot that is farthest forward is the

ABOUT THE NEXT 5 EXERCISES

Even though I have placed five backing up exercises all together (*Exercises 18 to 22*) in the same place here, I suggest you don't do a lot of backing up in one session. If you have a horse who has had a back injury or is on stall rest, ask your veterinarian if backing up is safe for your horse before starting one of these lessons. And when you do the exercises, you are not looking for hundreds of steps, just one perfect one. Once you can repeat that perfect step, time after time, then you can do as much or as little as you need.

diagonal that is going to move first. Make it easy for your horse by tipping his nose over that foot and asking him to step back, rewarding him, then tipping the nose the other way to get the other foot to step back. I'm not suggesting you "swing" the horse's head from one side to the other; just think about moving the lead rope a little so that his weight moves over the foot you want to move. (You may have a horse who always stops absolutely square. If that's so, you can choose which diagonal he's going to step with first.)

At this stage you're only looking at the front feet, but once you get a good first step with the front, you can start to ask with a bit more intention, and a bit more energy. Tip the horse's nose over the next front to move, lift your energy as if you were about to blow out a candle, and ask for that foot to step back. Position yourself so that you can see all four of his feet, watch when the feet move in diagonal pairs, and reward that moment. You're not going to reward anything else, just when the horse steps together in a diagonal pair. Let the horse know that he's got the right answer. Don't work hard at this; keep it short and

sweet. One good step is better than 10 mediocre ones.

As you get better at this, you'll find the backup has become soft without you ever having to work for it. This is because you are working with the horse both dynamically—by selecting the correct feet to move—and emotionally. You are not putting any pressure on him to be perfect every time. You are trying to make the communication between yourself and your horse subtle, so concentrate on keeping your own signals small.

WHAT IF

Many horses struggle with moving their legs in diagonal pairs going backward.

Don't worry, it's not imperative they do, but it's a great way to play with your horse's feet and see how you can influence their movement. Always remember, the horse may not be able to do this due to stiffness, pain, or injury, so always ask for professional help if you are not sure.

Timing is so important here; reward every correct step. Once the horse realizes he's doing the right thing by moving his legs in diagonal pairs, you'll find he'll be offering more often.

The ultimate aim with this exercise is to have the backup look like your horse is "trotting backward." When it doesn't, it isn't a proper backup, it's just the horse going backward.

Backing Up in a Circle and in a Straight Line

WHAT IT IS

If you can back your horse in a circle, you can back him in a straight line. Yes, it sounds crazy, but once you know how to back a horse in a circle, you know how to steer your horse, so you can steer him to go straight!

HOW TO DO IT

Draw a circle on the ground using shavings, a rope, or other safe markers. Don't make it too small to start with; you can get ambitious later. Position your horse on the marked circle and ask him to take a step back. For this exercise, you are aiming to keep the back feet roughly on the line of the circle you've marked out, and to be able to do that, you will need to steer them.

When you start to back in a circle,

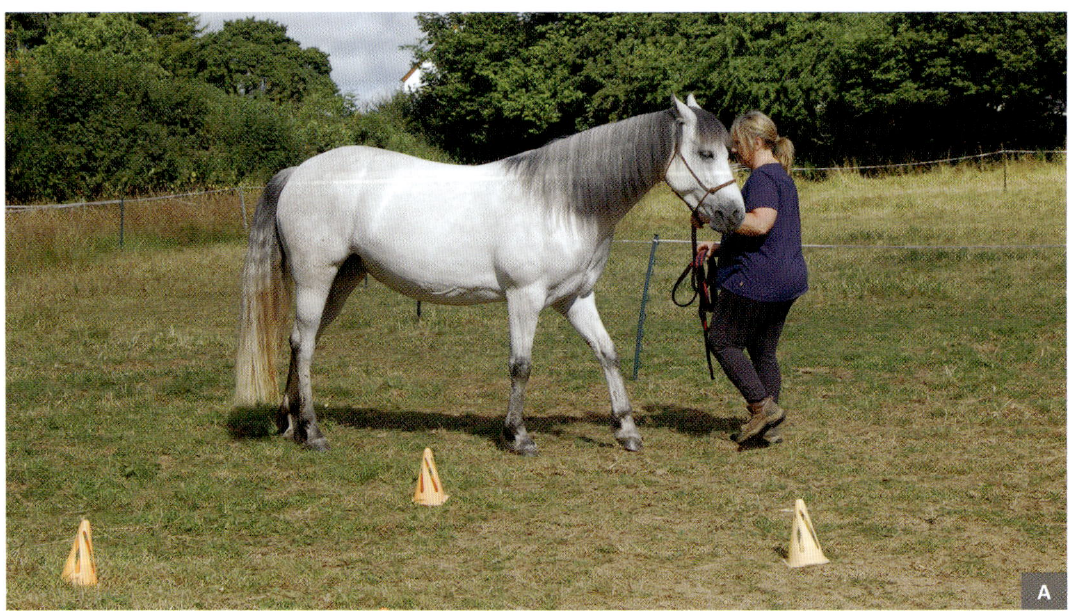

19 A & B Carol is preparing to ask Melody to step her right hind over to the right so that she can stay on the circle when backing up (A). The circle has been marked out using cones. Melody makes a nice step to the right with her right hind (B).

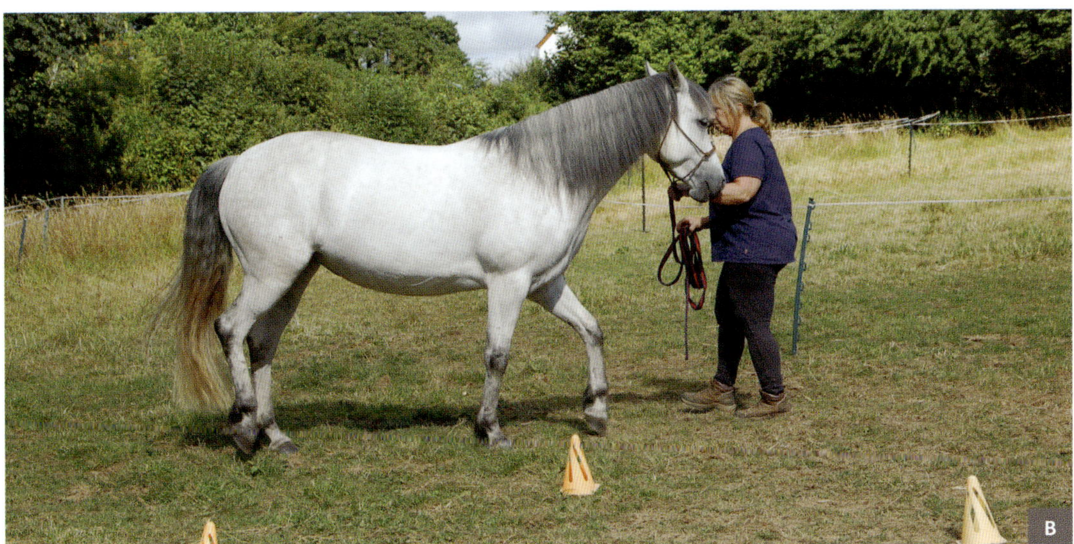

decide which direction you are going to need those hind feet to go. Try moving your horse's head so that he's almost (but not quite) looking over one shoulder. You will find that his hind end will move away from where he is looking, almost as if his head has pushed the hind end away (fig. 19 A).

Position the horse's head so he is looking to the outside of the circle. Ask him to take one step (fig. 19 B).

When the horse has taken a step, ask yourself, "Where are his hind feet on the circle?" When the hind feet are on the *outside* of the circle, you didn't turn the head far enough. When the feet are on the *inside* of the circle, you turned it too much. The horse's head has become like a steering wheel on a vehicle; how far you turn that head determines how far the hind end has moved over.

As you proceed backward, step by step, you will be deciding how far you need to move the horse's head, and the more you practice this, the more natural it will become, until you don't need to stop between steps and will be able to back up a complete circle without stopping at all. Remember to do this in both directions, clockwise and counterclockwise.

Next, take two poles and place them on the ground parallel to each other. You might want to make the distance between them wider at the beginning and lessen it as you

19 C Always make sure you use safe markers because some of them always get stepped on!

get better at steering in a straight line.

Lead your horse in between the poles until he is about halfway through, halt, and back him up through the poles without him stepping over or touching them. Because you now know how to steer your horse, you can make adjustments as you move backward to stay straight. When you get really good, you can do away with the poles and still back up in a perfectly straight line.

WHAT IF

If it's really not working, I usually find it's one of two things:

Pain can be a major reason why a horse finds backing up difficult, so do get professional advice. If your horse seems to be struggling, keep the sessions short—a quarter-circle is fine, or even less. Remember, you're not looking for a perfect circle, you're looking for a *correct step,* that's all.

The other reason people find this difficult is that they don't pause between steps, work out where they need to go next, and maneuver the horse accordingly. They just focus on "getting that circle done," and the error just gets bigger and bigger. So do slow down and assess each step at the beginning.

This is an advanced exercise, both physically and mentally, so don't overdo it. It is much better to get two perfect steps and leave it for the day.

Backing Up Over a Pole with the Front Feet

WHAT IT IS

This is a great exercise that helps you get in time with your horse's feet and read what he is going to do before he even moves them because of the way he is standing. The aim is to be able to lead your horse over a pole and halt so that the pole is under his belly. You need to decide which foot can move backward without the other foot moving. Then you are going to back him up over the pole so that his feet don't touch it (figs. 20 A & B).

If you're not quite sure what I mean by a foot not being able to move, try this:

- Stand up with your right foot forward and your left foot back. I'm going to ask you to take a step backward. You will start to lift your right foot because it's the easier one to move. You'll have rocked your weight onto the left foot to be able to do this.
- Suddenly I tell you: "No! Back up with your left!"

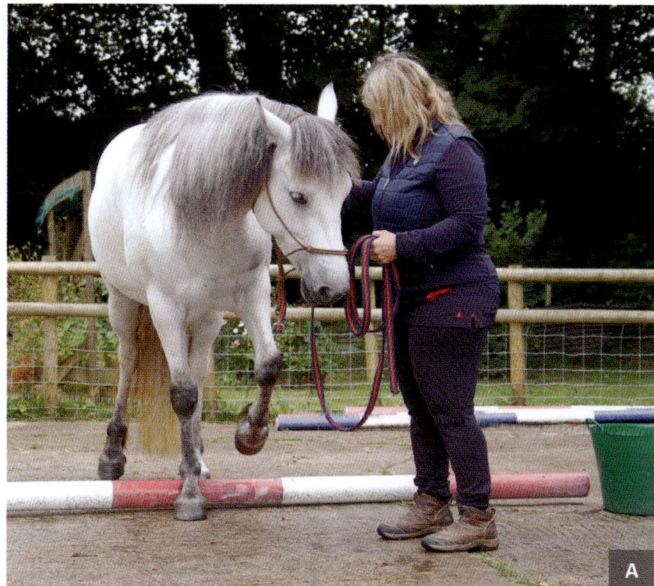

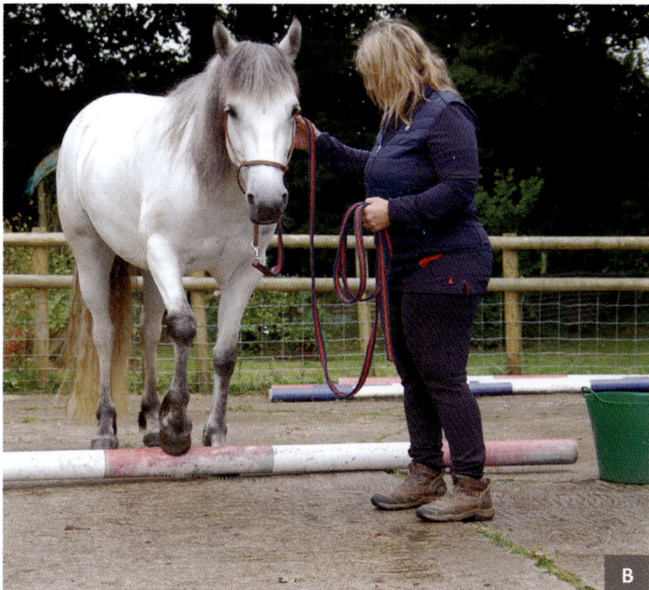

20 A & B Two nice soft steps backward over the pole.

■ There will be a moment of confusion—your weight is on the left foot, and the right foot may already be off the ground. You stamp the right foot down and try and lift your left foot up, but you will have to get the weight off the left and onto the right foot so you can even try and lift the left.

Would you be frustrated with the above scenario? Confused? I bet you would.

This happens to horses all the time because we ask them to move their feet without considering which foot is the next one that is naturally able to move. For example, we walk our horse over a pole and halt with the pole under his belly, and we want our horse to step his left foot back over the pole. But supposing his weight is on the left foot? Then he will try and answer our request by moving the right foot to free up the left. But we stop him, telling him that moving the right foot is the *wrong* answer, and we want the left foot to step back. The horse doesn't get it—he cannot move the left foot until he's moved the right one.

Is our horse frustrated? Confused? I bet he is.

Let's go back to you standing on two feet. When I asked you to step backward, you chose the easiest foot to move—the right one (the foot that was farther forward). If I wanted the left foot to move first, I needed to reposition your feet so that my request was easy for you to carry out. *Make the right thing easy.*

So, now that you have the theory, let's go back to the backup over a pole.

HOW TO DO IT

Put a pole on the ground; you may want to use something safe to stop it from rolling, such as sandbags or specialized pole holders.

Lead your horse over the pole and halt him as soon as his front feet are over the pole. The pole will be under his belly. Try to stop as soon as you can after he's stepped over (timing again!) because the fewer steps he has to take backward to reach the pole and step over it, the better. When you look at the way your horse is now standing after the halt, you will see that one front foot is farther forward than the other. This will be the foot to step back.

Ask him to take a step back with that foot (see *Exercise 10: Backing Up*, for help with this—p. 47); you don't want him to hit the pole, so raise your energy and your leading hand to encourage him to lift his

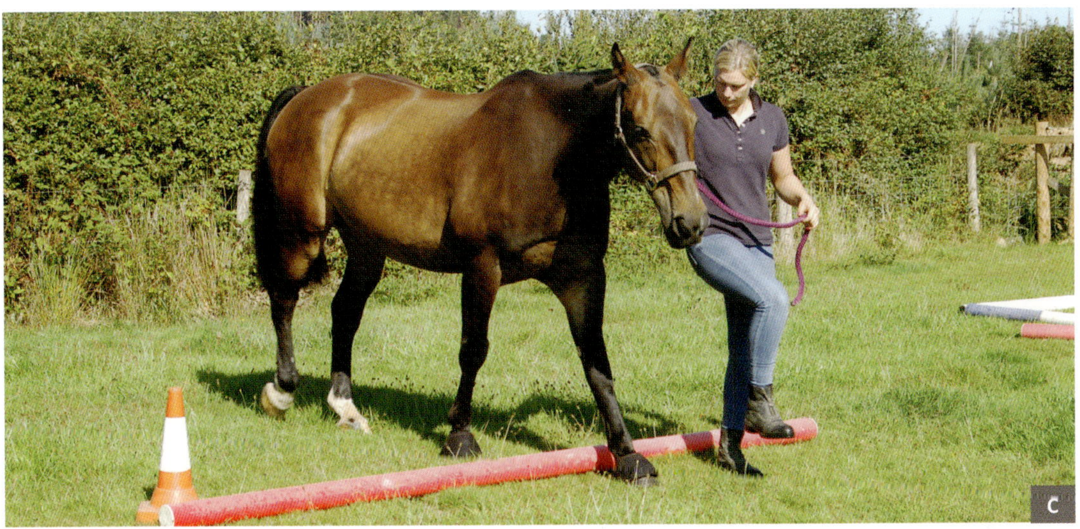

20 C Becky uses *synchronization (Exercise 11: Dancing Together,* p. 51) to help her horse understand how she wants him to step.

shoulder and hence his foot higher. Imagine you have a piece of string tied around that foot, and as it comes up off the ground, lift the imaginary rope as if you are lifting the foot up and back over the pole. This is all about practice, and more practice, and even more practice because it's about raising your energy before the foot has left the ground. By the time your energy has reached the horse, he's already committed to the lift, and you want to influence that lift before it's too late for the horse to change it.

This is also all about timing—getting in time with his feet.

Once you have helped the first foot to back up over the pole, you immediately need to think about the second foot, which is already getting ready to step backward. This is notoriously difficult because that second foot is preparing to lift just as the first foot reaches the ground on the other side of the pole, so you've got to be quick!

WHAT IF

I'm not going to pretend that this is an easy exercise. Feel and timing are what make great horse people. If you can play around with these ideas, I believe you'll really begin to realize how accurately you can influence the movement of the horse by getting in time with his feet and directing them to exactly where you want them to go (fig. 20 C).

EXERCISE 21
Backing Up Over a Pole with All Four Feet

WHAT IT IS

This is really an extension of *Exercise 20: Backing Up Over a Pole with the Front Feet* (p. 77) but much more challenging. A lot of people are used to moving their horse's *front* feet around on the ground but not the *back* feet. The principles for the front feet are exactly the same for lifting the hind feet over a pole.

HOW TO DO IT

Make sure you've had a bit of practice with backing the front feet over a pole before you start with all four feet (see p. 77). Even horses that have become good at cleanly stepping backward over a pole with the front feet sometimes struggle to do the same with the back feet, and the main reason is fear—fear of banging his legs on the pole.

The horse cannot see the pole because it's directly behind him, so if he needs to look over his shoulder (without stepping away to avoid the pole) then let him. Just

as before, when you lead him over the pole, make sure you halt him as soon as he's over it. Don't let him drift a long way from it—backing all four feet over a pole is a much more advanced technique than just the front feet (figs. 21 A & B). Ask him to back up, and as the hind foot is coming off the ground, lift your energy, imagine a rope is attached to the moving foot and you are lifting it up and over (see p. 79).

WHAT IF

I have seen this done thousands of times, as it is common in Horse Agility competitions. These are the mistakes I usually see:

- The handler unintentionally rewards the horse for knocking into the pole.
- The handler does not position the horse well enough to make it easy for him to back up over the pole.

So looking at the unintentional reason first:

Often when the horse knocks into the pole (forward or backward), the handler says, "Good boy!" or "Good girl!" I believe this is done to reassure the horse, but just

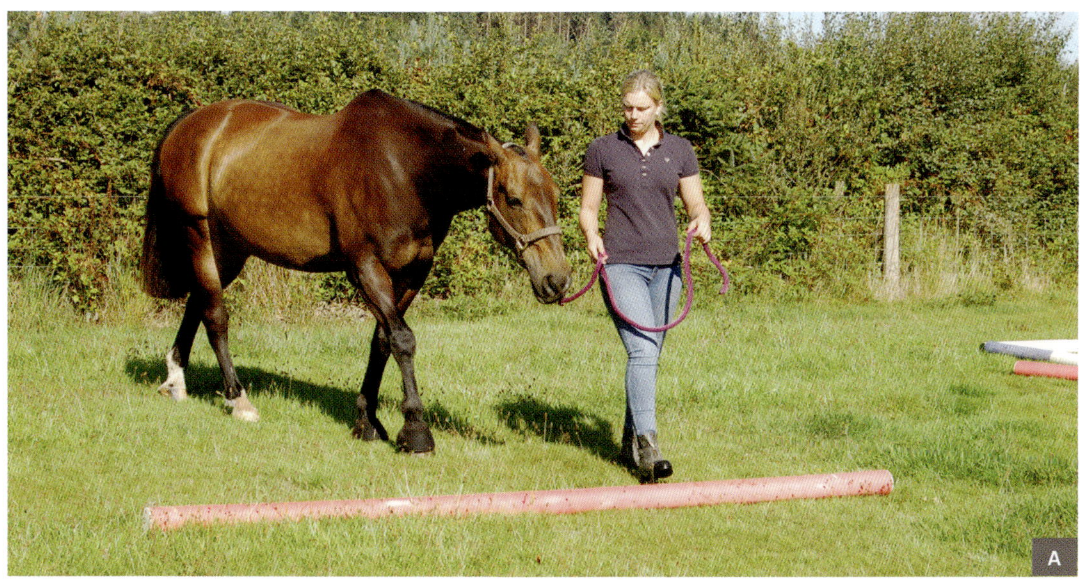

21 A & B Lead your horse over the pole first, and halt him as soon as all four feet have stepped over.

think what message that sends to the horse: "Knocking the pole is what she wants, so I'll do it again."

Ignoring the knock and really making a fuss when he *doesn't* hit the pole will help the horse work out what it is that gets a positive response.

Now let's look at pole presentation.

Get on all fours (if you can), and crawl over a pole or similar, and stop on the other side. Now try to back up over the pole. Quite quickly, you will see that you must arrange your "feet" so you don't hit the pole. In other words, if you're too close as you lift your "foot" it will touch the pole, and if you are too far away you will also touch the pole because you have to stretch or shorten the step to try and accommodate the pole, and this takes a lot of practice.

When you work out the perfect position for the horse's feet, you can set it up from the start to make it easy for him to back up over the pole. Really "put yourself into the horse's shoes." Walk on two legs and on all fours over a pole, both forward and backward. What do you have to do so that you don't touch it? If every time you backed up over the pole *without* touching it, I gave you something nice (glass of wine, chocolate, money?), I bet you'd get pretty good at missing that pole! Remember, the horse hasn't got a clue what you want him to do. Most of the time, he's just trying out all possible answers to see what gets the reward. So make it easy for him. Acknowledge the answer you *want*, and ignore everything else!

EXERCISE 22
Backing in a Figure Eight

WHAT IT IS

The figure-eight pattern is a very powerful way of finding out which of the horse's feet doesn't move as freely as all the others. Later, you'll be looking at how you can develop the figure-eight pattern when walking (*Exercise 29: The Figure Eight—* p. 104), but here's a good place to have a look at the figure-eight backup. You can make the figure eight very big at the start, but the aim here is eventually to make it as small as you can so that every step has to be precise to stay within the pattern.

HOW TO DO IT

You will need two markers to place on the ground. Two cones or plastic bucket lids

22 A Becky is steering Archie's feet in a figure eight around two cones.

work fine—anything safe, because you'll be amazed how often the horse will step on them as you steer him in reverse.

Place the markers about two horse-lengths apart (a horse-length is the length of his body). Don't get too ambitious to begin. The markers are the middle of each "circle" of the figure eight. Don't cheat and try to do it without the markers because you really want to aim for accuracy here. You are going to ask your horse to back around the markers in a figure eight pattern.

From *Exercise 19: Backing Up in a Circle and in a Straight Line* (p. 74) you now

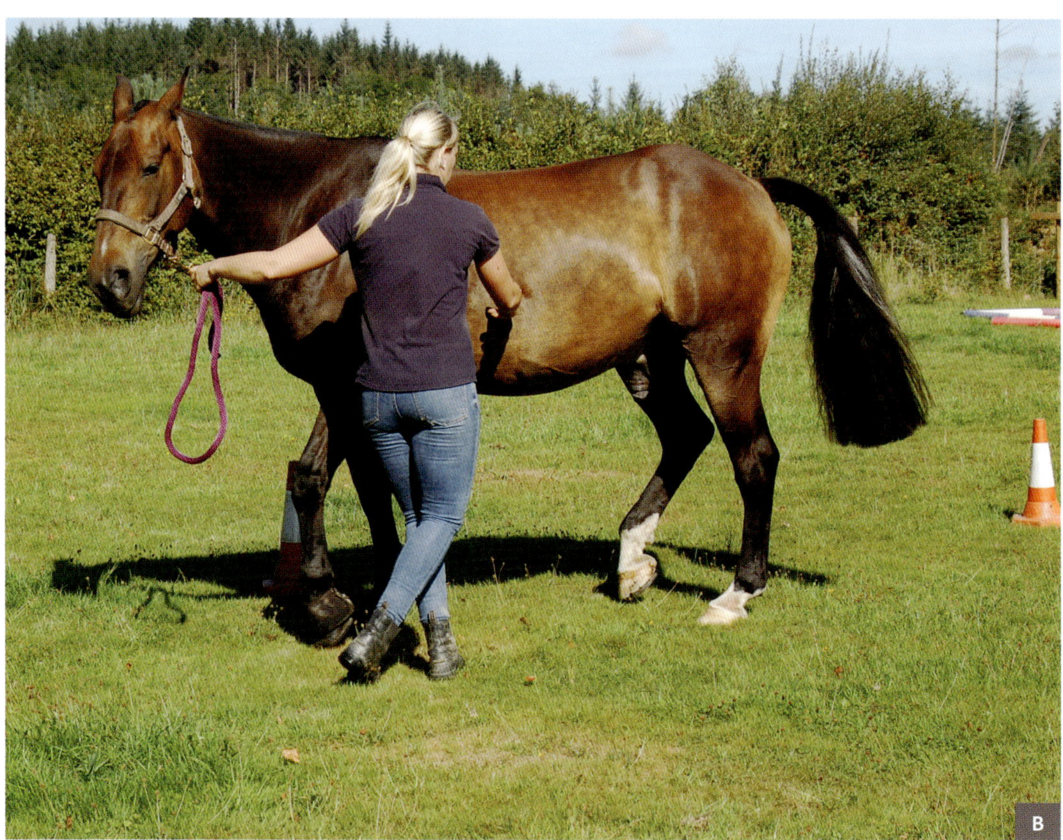

22 B She needs to steer every foot and keep changing sides to direct him.

know how to steer backward. Just work on one step at a time and forget the bigger picture of a seamless figure eight with no stops or bulges. Assess each step, and see exactly where you need the horse to put his feet next. I find it easier to "draw" the pattern on the ground with shavings or sand, and then try to stick to that line.

WHAT IF

When it all starts going off the figure-eight pattern with, perhaps, a large circle at one end and a tiny one the other, or the horse is constantly stepping on the markers, stop. You are going too fast. Look for one good step, pause, look for another good step. It's a good way of learning the sequence of footfalls because you will need to work out which foot is going to move next.

Your aim, eventually, is to back in "two-time"—so those diagonal legs move together in pairs. This will be difficult at the start so don't worry about that aspect, just get the backup on the line of the figure eight. You can imagine if two legs are moving together and you're steering the horse, the legs are going to be moving in quite different ways, unlike the straight backup where the legs move in the same direction and with the same length of stride.

For a bit of fun, why not get on all fours and try going backward with the opposite leg and arm moving backward together? Now, try and back around a corner. Not easy, is it? Imagine someone else is steering you. Give the horse, and yourself, time to learn how this works.

EXERCISE 23
Moving Sideways

WHAT IT IS

Being able to move your horse sideways is a useful skill, both on the ground and under saddle. Think about opening and closing gates on a ride and loading into a slant-load trailer. Both require the horse to move sideways at some point.

Just as in the backup, a true sideways is when the diagonal pairs of legs step together. One sequence could be this: The right front leg steps out to the side and the left hind leg crosses over the right hind leg under the belly (fig. 23 A). Then the left front leg crosses over the right front leg at the same time as the right hind steps out to the side (fig. 23 B).

It's really "trotting sideways."

HOW TO DO IT

You may need to refer to *Exercises 12 and 13: Moving the Hind End Around* and *Moving the Front End Around* (pp. 54 and 57) to find out how to move the front and

the back separately. To start the sideways movement, ask the front end to step away, then ask the back end to step away, and repeat. At this point, you could put in a vocal cue such as, "Over," or "Sideways." As the horse begins to realize there's a pattern—front end over, back end over, front end over, and so on—he'll start to move both ends almost at the same time.

Now comes the clever part: start to move your hand nearer to the middle of

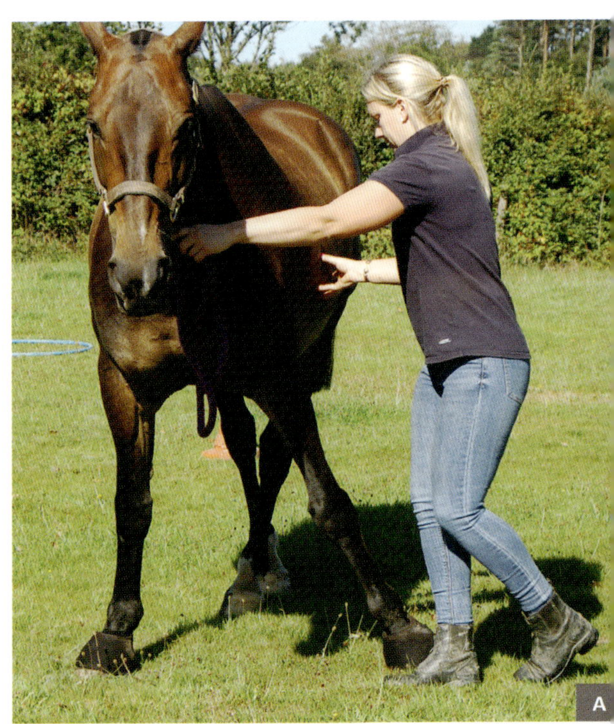

the horse's body with each ask. When you are pressing on the neck to get the front to move over, start to move your hand back toward the shoulder. And when you are touching the hip to get the horse to step his hind end over, start to move your hand along his belly. You are moving the position of the touch so that eventually the touch will merge into one point, which will be the "middle" of the horse, and when you touch this spot, he will know to move sideways away from you. This isn't going to happen overnight. Slowly build up this skill, and always stop when it's going well.

WHAT IF

The most common problem is that the horse tries to walk forward. In the early training sessions, I suggest you face the horse into a wall or fence so that he can't go forward. Don't put too much pressure on him. To do this perfectly, there's a lot for the horse to think about, as well as for you, so go slowly. Sometimes walking the horse over a pole and halting him so that the pole is under is belly helps him stay straight as he steps sideways along the pole (fig. 23 C).

One direction will be easy and the other more difficult. Don't worry; just look for the smallest try in the horse that

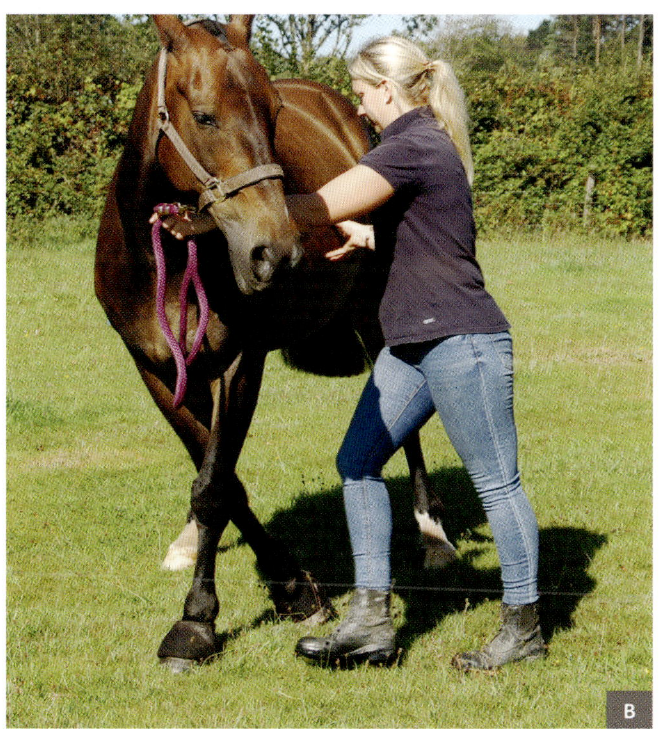

23 A & B Right front and left hind stepping together. Note the position of Becky's hand on Archie's side (A). Left front and right hind stepping together (B).

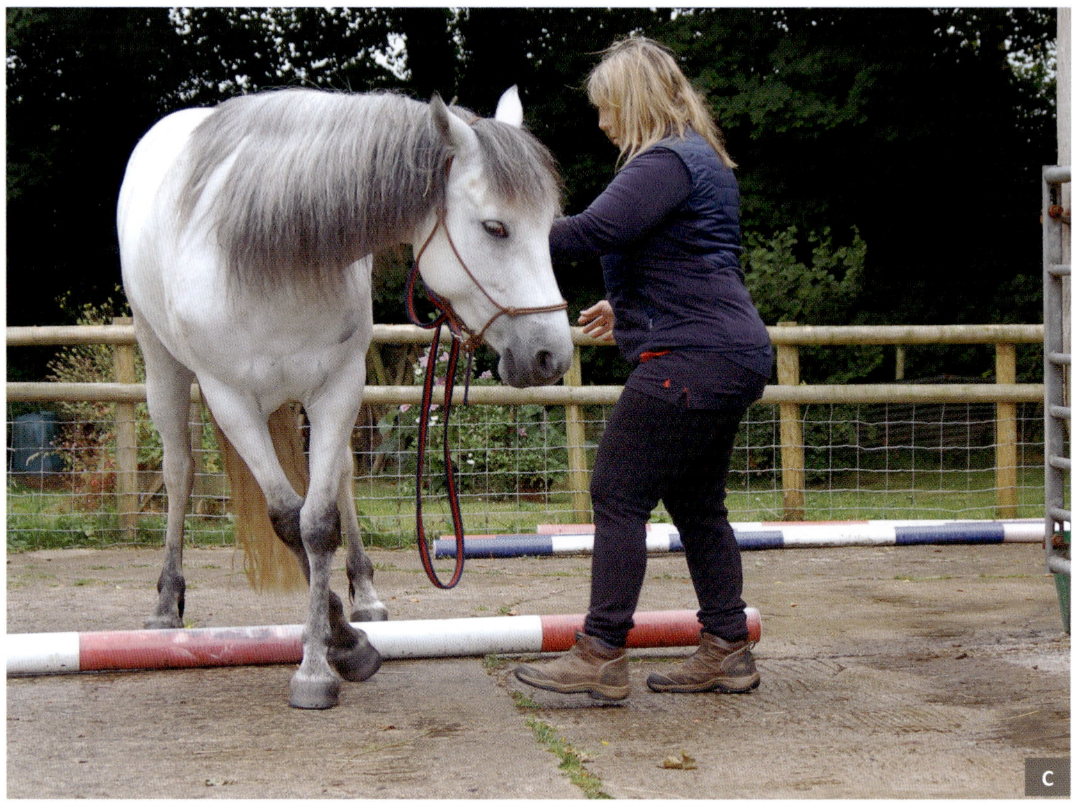

23 C Carol uses a pole to help keep the "sideways" as straight as possible with no movement forward or backward.

shows he's doing his best. Horses don't do a lot of sideways naturally so it may be completely new to him.

Be aware of your horse's reaction to this exercise because if he's not used to stepping sideways, it could wake up some muscles he doesn't use very often and feel uncomfortable. Look for tail-swishing, ears back, and his head coming round to you—in those cases, do less. Stop if you're not sure and seek professional help, because there could be a physical issue that doesn't show up in any other movement.

EXERCISE 24
Changing Sides

WHAT IT IS

This is a fun way of asking your horse to move to the other side of you without you moving your feet—he does all the walking. This can be useful when saddling or grooming him, and done well, it is an elegant, free-flowing movement.

HOW TO DO IT

Stand beside your horse, and start on the off side of him. Ask him to walk forward around you (fig. 24 A), and as he does, ask him to step his hind end away so that his head comes toward you (fig. 24 B). He will end up facing you but still moving around

24 A Lesley asks Daisy to walk round in front of her by lifting the lead rope and pointing in the direction she wants her horse to go.

24 B–D As Daisy walks past, Lesley brings Daisy's head around to face her by putting a little tension in the lead rope—not a pull (B)! Daisy turns around (C) and walks up to join Lesley on the other side (D).

you, walking a small circle. As he moves, you will begin to see the opposite side of the horse. Ask him to continue walking around to join you on the other side (figs. 24 C & D).

This should be one smooth movement with no pulling on the head. The horse turns to face you after a half-circle around you before straightening up to stand beside you on the near side.

You can also do this while you are moving forward. It's a fun exercise!

WHAT IF

When this exercise isn't working, break it down into the separate movements I mention, and get each one solid on its own before you put them all together. As with many of the following exercises, there are quite a few skills needed.

Downpour

EXERCISE 25
Getting Used to Umbrellas

WHAT IT IS

The exercises in this section might take a little longer than the previous ones, and you will really need to observe your horse for signs of fear or discomfort. Some of these exercises can be quite challenging (and even scary) for him, so don't assume anything and don't rush. As with all the lessons in this book, stop for the day when it's done well, or move onto another exercise. Keep the session short and interesting.

I once heard a well-known horseman remark that it was a waste of time getting horses used to umbrellas as they hardly ever saw them. The following week, he happened to be competing outside in a dressage competition, and halfway through his test, a light shower of rain crossed the arena. The spectators, sitting along the fence line, grabbed their umbrellas and with a click and a rustle opened them up. Chaos ensued as the horse refused to move along the long side where those terrifying umbrellas had suddenly appeared. The rider retired and left the arena red-faced. Over the next week, he spent some time teaching his horses that umbrellas were not going to eat them. He never had that problem again.

HOW TO DO IT

Start small, and gradually increase what you are asking the horse to accept (figs. 25 A–D). The last thing you need to do is just open the umbrella and see what happens. What happens may be far more than you bargained for!

Begin with the umbrella closed and rolled up, and let the horse explore it. Make sure you keep any sharp ends away from the horse so he doesn't poke his eyes.

If he's a bit wary of the closed umbrella, try walking forward with him while you hold the umbrella in front of you so that

25 A & B Let your horse safely explore the umbrella when it is closed (A). Open it a little so the material begins to move and perhaps rustle (B).

he's almost "chasing the umbrella away." When you stop walking, you'll find that he'll most likely be more interested and less wary, and reach out toward the closed umbrella.

The next stage is to unfurl the umbrella a little so that it's just a bit flappy. Don't put it up yet; just let it rustle and move so it looks less like a stick and changes shape

25 C & D Carol is rubbing the umbrella on Melody's back, but you can see here that the horse is not comfortable with this yet (C). Be careful when you open the umbrella. Try to do it slowly and smoothly, as Carol is doing here (D).

when you move it. Again, let the horse explore this new object safely.

Now, very slowly and gently, put the umbrella up. Don't dramatically press the clip so that it "explodes" upward! This needs to be done quietly. Keep the umbrella at eye level: holding it low to the ground makes it look more like a predator, ready to pounce.

Hold the open umbrella away from the horse—don't offer it to him, just let him look. Because you know your horse, you will see if he is afraid, curious, or comfortable with it. When he's afraid, just quietly close the umbrella and give him a bit of peace. Then open it slowly again. The second time he will be less concerned because last time, it didn't attack him. Keep quietly and gently opening and closing the umbrella, taking a long time for each movement. Any fast or sharp motions at this stage could cause him to try to leave, and you're trying to help him realize he doesn't need to.

Once he's happy with this, lead him with the umbrella in the open position, being careful to keep it away from his eyes and mouth. Offer the umbrella to the horse, and when he shows curiosity, take it away. This will increase his interest in it.

The next stage is for someone else to do all the above steps a small distance away. Your horse might be very brave when he sees that *you're* in charge of the umbrella, but what if someone else is? Most horses do seem to struggle with an opened umbrella moving along seemingly on its own, almost like a walking giant mushroom, so I recommend you ask for help exposing him to this.

Try this tip: every mealtime, approach your horse's stall carrying an open umbrella, put it down, and then feed him. This way, he will begin to associate umbrellas with something good.

WHAT IF

With some horses, getting comfortable with umbrellas can be a slow process, but I find it interesting to work in such tiny slices of knowledge that the horse never shows fear, just a little wariness. This requires time and patience, but even if you only have a few minutes, you can still complete one of your tiny slices and build the confidence of the horse. It helps to make a written list of all baby steps; in some tasks such as this one, there could be a lot!

Flag Waving

WHAT IT IS

It doesn't matter if you go to horse shows, ride on trails, or work in an arena; somewhere along the way you'll come across a flag or two. The thing about a flag is that, unlike an opened umbrella, the flag's shape is constantly changing as the breeze moves it around.

HOW TO DO IT

Find yourself a flag or make one out of a piece of material, and attach it to a light cane. Don't use anything heavy, because you could be holding and waving it for quite some time.

I like to approach flag training in two ways:

- First, I move the horse to the flag.
- Second, I move the flag to the horse.

To start with, attach your flag to a fence or post. If it's a windy day, you can roll or tie up the flag so there's not too much move-ment. To stay safe, always ensure you are next to the flag. Should the horse spook, he

will jump away from the flag, and you won't be run over.

With your flag secured, lead your horse around the area near the flag, first getting closer to it, then moving farther away. It's as if you're just wandering around, taking no notice of the flag at all. Don't go marching up to the flag straightaway. Your attitude needs to be that you are just out for a walk, and the flag is not of any interest at all. Resist focusing on the flag and instead give an air of nonchalance.

Keep moving around, ensuring you, not the horse, are always nearest the flag, and the horse is on the outside, *away* from the flag. If your horse starts pulling away from the flag, you've gone too fast, so walk farther away for a moment, and then begin to move in but much more slowly. You may need to end that session because the horse's adrenaline will be up, and it's impossible to help a horse become brave when he's already afraid.

Once your horse can be led near the flag

26 A & B You can try walking with your horse as he "chases" the flag away (A). You can even start to wave it about so that it changes shape (B).

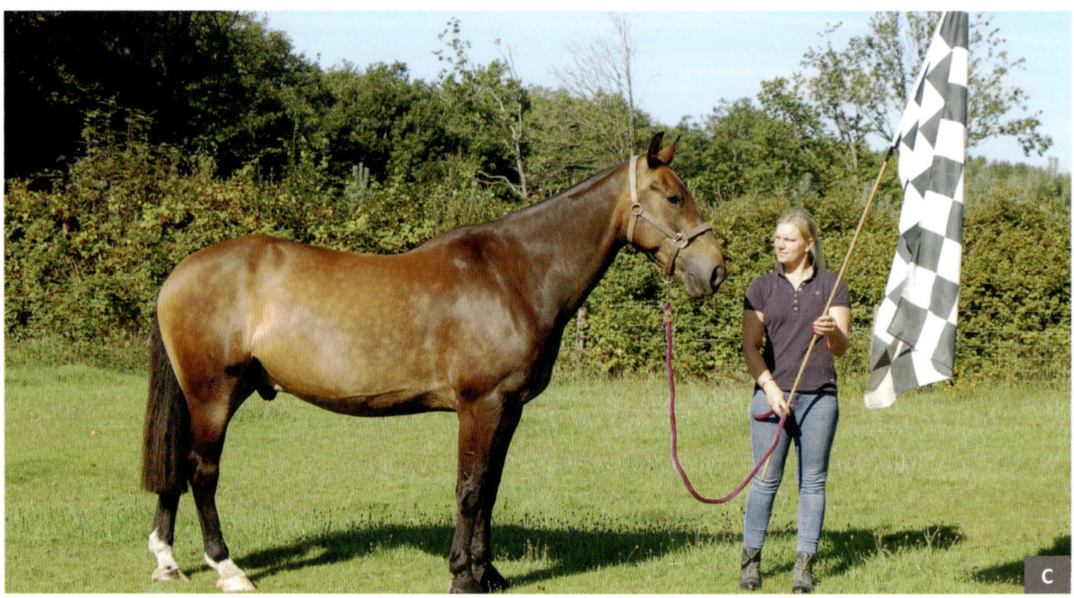

26 C You can see that Archie isn't completely happy with the flag and more work is needed to help him.

without feeling he needs to leave, you can start to move the flag to him. I find walking your horse forward, holding the flag in front of you (as with *Exercise 25*—p. 92) is a great place to start. With some horses you may need to roll the flag up to start with and slowly let it out; it depends on how windy it is that day. Just as with the umbrella, offering the flag to the horse and moving it away when he shows interest is a great way to increase his curiosity (figs. 26 A–C).

WHAT IF

Some people put a flag up in their horse's field or paddock to help him get used to it, but when your horse is really scared, this would be very unfair. Put yourself in such a situation. For example, imagine you are frightened of spiders and someone decides you shouldn't be. Suppose they put you in a room with a big hairy spider. Would you get braver? Probably not. It's more likely to make you more scared than ever.

Once your horse is comfortable with a flag in one place you can start to change its position. With the flag moving from one place to another, he will learn that flags can turn up anywhere!

EXERCISE 27
Weaving Through Cones

WHAT IT IS

In this exercise you're starting to think about the cues you are going to use to direct your horse to move away and come back to you without using the lead rope. This is because you want the horse to move freely and without any force or tension on the rope, which would influence the fluidity of his movement. The cue can be vocal ("Come here" and "Go away"), body language such as a hand signal (pointing in the direction you want your horse to go), or your body moving toward and away from the horse. You can experiment and find what works for you and your horse.

HOW TO DO IT

Set out a few cones in a straight line—five is a good number. They need to be about

27 A A nice loose lead rope as Becky and Archie start the weave.

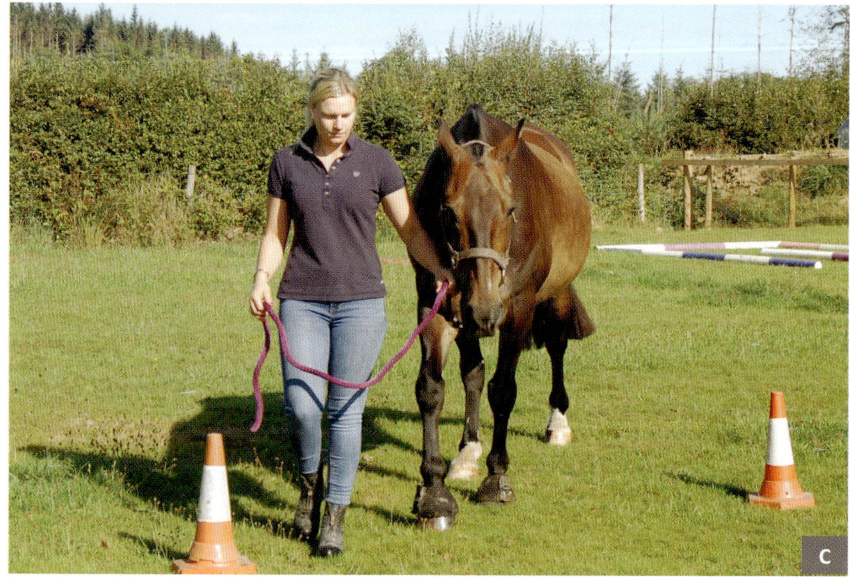

27 B & C With an obvious step away but not pulling on the rope, Becky invites Archie to move toward her (B). Once he can do a nice weave on one side, why not try leading from the other side (C)?

two horse-lengths apart. Don't put them too close together. It might seem that making the weave shorter would give your horse less room to go wrong, but because he has to turn more sharply with a tight weave, he will almost be facing away from you in the turn, and that isn't a good place to start.

Decide on the cues you are going to use, experiment, and find what you are comfortable with. It really doesn't matter what you use, but it's absolutely paramount that you use the same cues each time. You can't say "Come" in one session then "Come here" the next time because the horse won't understand. Consistency is key to him being able to respond the way you want.

Once you've set your cones up, walk beside your horse somewhere between his head and his shoulder and lead him through the cones, trying to keep a nice loose lead rope (figs. 27 A–C). You want him to be able to see you and be aware of the cues you are giving him for "Go away" and "Come here." You will be weaving together through the cones, and using this to introduce your chosen cues to steer him through. Practice this a few times and he will begin to connect the action with the cue.

Now you are going to walk *beside* the cones, *not* weaving, while the horse is going to weave. Stay in your position between his head and shoulder, and use your chosen cues to ask him to weave by going away from and coming back to you around the five cones. Horses get this very quickly, but it is important you don't go too far away from him. Don't use the lead rope to bring him back to you because you want him to respond to your "Come here" signal, not the rope.

WHAT IF

The main problem here is when people are not consistent with their cues. They also create too big a distance between them and the horse so the horse loses the connection. Once you and your horse can do this at walk, why not try trotting, and then, perhaps, canter? The important thing is to establish those cues. I cannot stress that enough.

Send Your Horse Away and Around a Marker

WHAT IT IS

You already have the cues you need in place if you have worked through *Exercise 27: Weaving Through Cones* (p. 99). You have the cues to "Go away" and "Come here." You can use a lead rope with this exercise if you wish, but don't rely on it, because it's fun to send a horse a really long way out and ask him to come back, and you won't have a lead rope long enough when you get really good at it!

HOW TO DO IT

This is all about being able to send the horse away and then recalling him when you need him to come back to you. I always suggest the handler stands in a hula hoop or on a bucket lid to help her keep her feet still.

Place a cone or another marker a short distance away from you, and, using your "Go away" cue, ask your horse to walk away from you, toward the marker. You are sending him away (fig. 28 A). I find that pointing works

here—I draw the path I want him to walk with my finger. I picked this idea up from doing dog agility with my Greyhound.

When the horse reaches the cone, ask him to come back. This is the *recall*. You'll find he'll walk around the cone to return to you. Remember, the distance is

28 A–C Carol asks Melody to walk round a bucket, keeping the distance short to start with (A). She increases the distance and asks Melody to pick up the pace (B). Melody decides to experiment with a new answer to Carol's request to walk round the bucket (C)!

only a few feet on the first tries; don't send him too far. Move the cone a few inches farther away and repeat (fig. 28 B). When you feel ready, take the lead rope off. Don't change anything—act as if that rope is still attached.

WHAT IF

As always, it's easy to keep moving on when it's going well, but in fact it's better to stop and have a break when it's going well, even if your horse tries out a few different ideas (fig. 28 C). If the horse starts cutting in front of the cone, you've moved it too far, too quickly. Horses seem to have a distance particular to them where they suddenly appear to lose confidence and become lost. All horses vary, but do be aware of that moment when you feel like the connection between you has broken, and come back to where it was good. This distance just needs to be gently extended.

EXERCISE 29
The Figure Eight

WHAT IT IS

The Figure Eight starts with simple leading in a figure-eight pattern around two markers, and leads on to something I call the *Remote Figure Eight,* where the handler stands still and sends the horse around the two markers on his own. The last *Exercise 28: Send Your Horse Away and Around a Marker* (p. 102) will really help with this one. You need to be able to send and recall your horse from both sides, which for some may be quite interesting. You can see in the photographs that Ricky did not find this an easy exercise. He is tense and pulling on the rope. If your horse is like this, remain quiet and calm and stop when it's done well.

HOW TO DO IT

Place two markers on the ground. They can be cones or anything safe to mark the center of each circle of the figure eight.

Establish the pattern by leading your horse around the cones by walking with him. You will find there will be places in the pattern where he will slow down and

perhaps not feel so free to lead. Keep walking the pattern with him until he feels easy to lead all the way around and in both directions (figs. 29 A–G).

Next, stand away from the cones and position your horse on the other side of the cones, facing you through the gap. You know how to send your horse around things from the previous exercise (p. 102) so ask him to go around the cone on your left and come toward you.

Before he reaches you, send his front end away to walk round the second cone that is on your right. He will walk around that cone and come back to you.

Before he reaches you, ask him to go

29 A–E **A nice loose rope and a good bend in Ricky to take the turn around the first cone (A), and a good position to take the turn around the second (B). I ask Ricky to walk around the first cone again (C). The rope is tighter than I would like to see. Off he goes around the first cone (D). I change hands on the rope and ask Ricky to walk between the two cones (E).**

29 F & G Then he walks around the second cone and is about to face me (F). Finally, he walks between the cones to start the whole sequence again (G).

around the first cone again and repeat the pattern. You are trying to keep your feet as still as possible, though, of course, to start with, you'll probably want to move them around a bit. If you've got a lead rope on, think about changing hands on the rope when he changes direction so that he has plenty of room to move without having to pull on the rope.

WHAT IF

This normally starts to go wrong because people haven't mastered the *send* and *recall* explained in *Exercise 28: Send Your Horse Away and Around a Marker* (p. 102). But I promise, if you keep it calm and slow, you'll be able to do this at canter with a flying change in the middle one day—just not at the start!

EXERCISE 30
Crossing a Tarpaulin

WHAT IT IS

This is the first obstacle I work with when I meet a new horse. It's safe because there is plenty of room for the horse and handler to keep away from each other and nothing to trip over. Asking your horse to move over different surfaces at your request is invaluable when you ride out on the trail or go to shows. My mare always found any changes on a road surface worrying, and it took some time for her to realize a puddle wouldn't swallow her and the white lines on the road weren't some sort of fence to clear.

HOW TO DO IT

I use a heavyweight tarpaulin or a square of thick carpet. I don't like those very light-woven tarpaulins because they can shred and a horse's shoe or foot can get caught up in the holes.

Your horse will either walk straight over the tarpaulin or he won't, but by now, you'll know how fearful he is because you've been watching for those little signs we talked about in *Exercise 2: Observing Something New* (p. 19). The very last thing you want to do is try to force him. I've had horses absolutely refuse to even look at the tarp and walk around it with their heads twisted away so they can't see it.

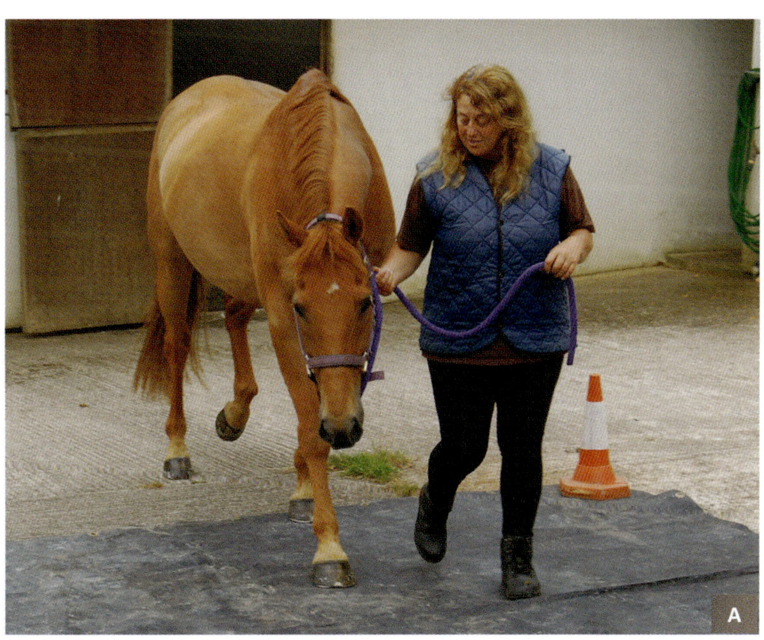

30 A Rachel has a nice loose lead rope and walks confidently over the tarpaulin with Memphis.

30 B & C Teri lets Breeze investigate the tarpaulin (B). Breeze wants to use his foot to test the tarpaulin, so Teri stands calmly by as he checks out the different surface (C).

I find the simplest way of getting a reluctant horse to walk across a tarpaulin is to absolutely ignore the tarpaulin, just as I recommended in *Exercise 26: Flag Waving* (p. 96). I walk around the area, leading my horse, and sometimes I just happen to walk on the tarpaulin, and sometimes I don't. I wander about but all the time I'm keeping an eye on the horse. At some point, he will look at the tarpaulin. Timing is everything here, so as soon as I see this look, I turn and walk *away* from the tarpaulin. I just keep doing this, and it's amazing how quickly the horse will pull *toward* the tarpaulin, asking to go and look at it.

This is when I join him in this curiosity, and we both go and inspect the new surface (figs. 30 A–C). I wander onto the tarp, and I wander off it. It's all very casual. If he needs to sniff or paw it, I just let him get on with it. At no time have I asked the horse to walk on the tarpaulin. I'm ready when he decides he would like to walk onto it because he may get halfway across and jump off or he may run over it—I just make sure I am not in the way. The important thing here is that the *horse* makes the decision to walk across, not me. I feel this empowers him.

WHAT IF

Sometimes the horse will paw at the tarp, even bunching it up and trampling on it. This is fine—let him explore. If you can change the color or texture of the tarpaulin or carpet in another session, so much the better; the more he experiences in life, the more confident he will become.

If your horse walks straight across the tarpaulin, you can start to ask him to stop on it, back off it, back over it, or maybe turn a circle on it. When you're doing these more advanced maneuvers, it is a good idea to have a heavyweight tarp so it doesn't wrap around his legs.

EXERCISE 31
Working without a Lead Rope

WHAT IT IS

This is a fun way of starting to work with your horse without a lead rope attached. Some people call it "liberty." In *Exercise 27: Weaving Through Cones* (p. 99), you started to pin down what cues you were going to use to direct a horse to weave through a line of five cones without moving through with him yourself. When you get this solid, you can start to think about taking the lead rope off. If you are always used to using a lead rope, taking it off may seem a distant dream or even impossible, but using a rope around the neck is a great way to get started.

If you've been careful not to use the lead rope to direct your horse in the weave, then you're all set up to get going with this exercise. You want the horse to be responding to your vocal cues or body language because the aim is to get rid of the rope, and if you keep using it, the horse will rely on it and be lost when it isn't there.

HOW TO DO IT

Have a look back at *Exercise 27: Weaving Through Cones* (p. 99) and set up your five cones or other markers in a straight line. Don't put them too close together because it makes the exercise much more difficult; you can try that challenge when you get really good at the first steps.

Make sure you are working in a safe area with the doors or gates closed in case your horse wanders away. Using the rope loop round the horse's neck (figs. 31 A & B) or just a halter without a lead rope, when you feel ready, start to ask your horse to weave through the cones. Use exactly the same cues as you did before. Don't change anything, pretend he still has that rope attached to the halter, and off you go.

WHAT IF

The main problem I encounter here is that people change their cues when they take the rope off. It's not a conscious thing; I think we're all so used to being attached to our horse that when we haven't got a rope on him, we feel out of control. As long as you are working in a safe, enclosed space, what could go wrong? He could wander off, but

31 A & B Lesley is using a long rope made into loop that she has put around Daisy's neck (A). The rope has a knot in it to stop the loop from becoming tight around her throat. Should Daisy pull away, the rope cannot choke her (you can see the knot at Daisy's right shoulder in B). Lesley is using good body language to request Daisy's attention without using the rope.

all that means is that he needs more time to understand the cues you've chosen, that's all. When you are working the horse at liberty and your horse leaves you, it's normally because you have relied on the rope too much and your cues just need to be a bit more solid.

EXERCISE 32
More Work without a Lead Rope

WHAT IT IS

This is an extension of *Exercise 31: Working without a Lead Rope* (p. 110) because it's always best to give variety in these exercises. If you've made some good progress with weaving through cones without a lead rope, it's time to try some of the obstacles you played with back when it was only a passing "shower" (see p. 51).

HOW TO DO IT

Have a look back at *Exercise 16: Squeezing Through a Narrow Gap* (p. 65). You asked the horse to wait while you went through the gap, then asked the horse to join you.

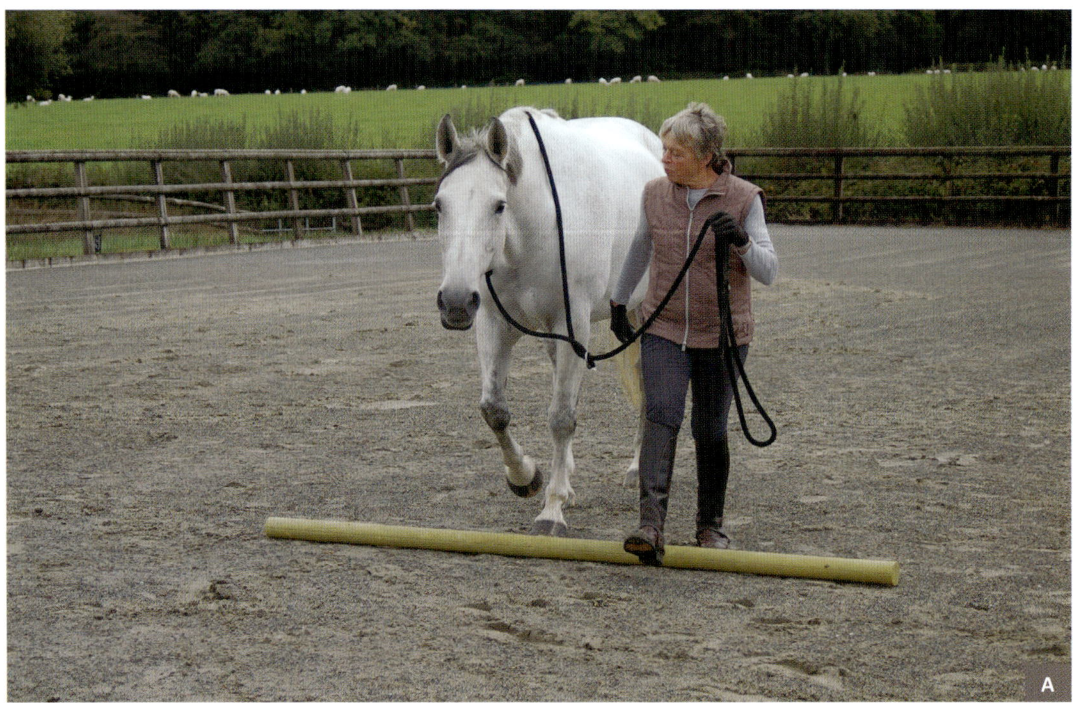

32 A & B You can start to add in a few simple obstacles, like these poles.

For that you needed to have a good "Wait" cue established (see *Exercise 8*—p. 38). Can you see how everything is linked together? If there is an exercise you are doing well with the lead rope attached, now try it with the rope *off* (figs. 32 A–C). This is like a little test of how strong that cue to "Wait" really is.

Other exercises you can try while the horse is loose are *Exercise 17: Going Under Something Low* (p. 66) and *Exercise 30: Crossing a Tarpaulin* (p. 107).

WHAT IF

The lesson about taking the lead rope off is that you're only left with the truth. You might *think* you aren't relying on that rope, but when you take it off and the horse immediately moves away, it tells you that your connection is broken. Wouldn't it be

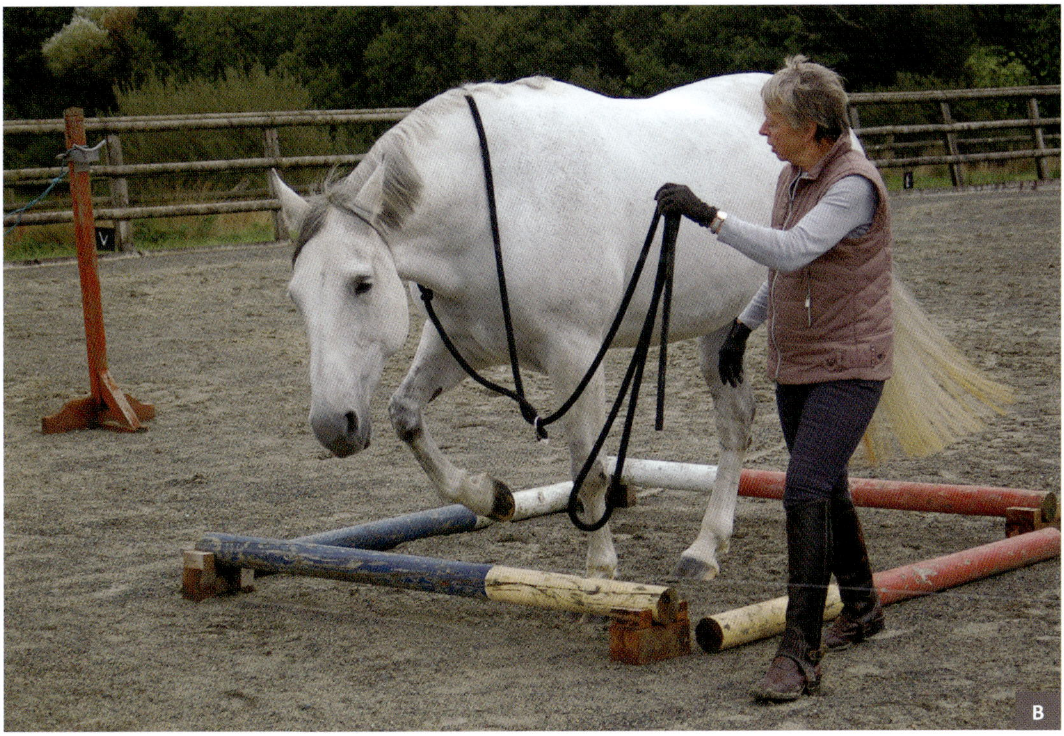

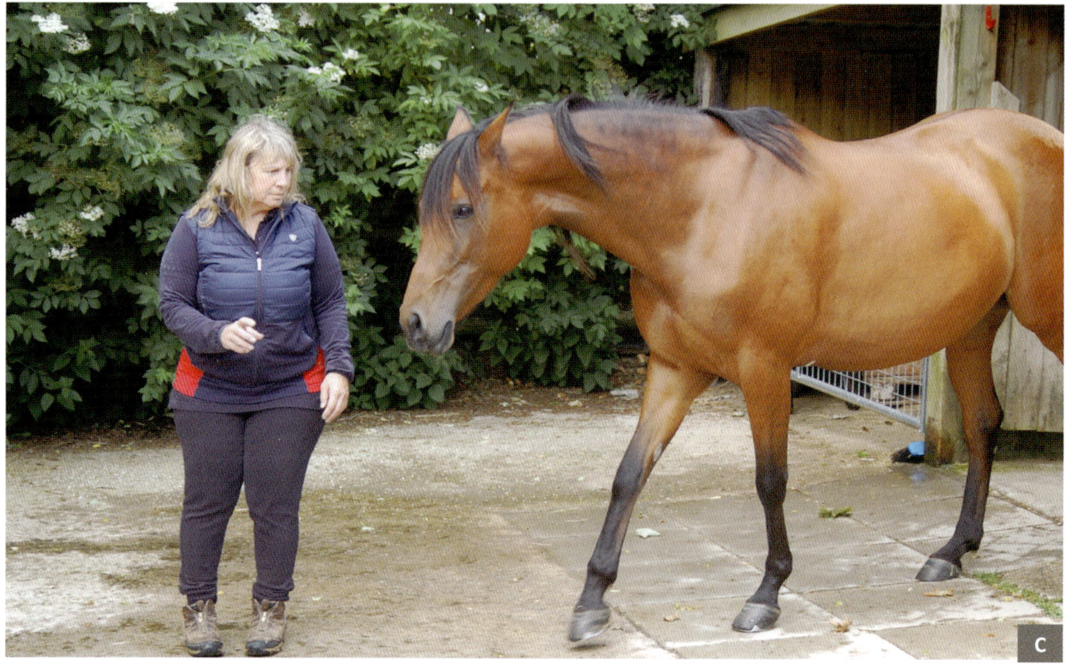

32 C Carol works at liberty with Libby in a safe area using the smallest cues. Here she is asking Libby to bring her right foot forward and place it on the ground.

wonderful if you could keep that communication going even when the horse has the choice to leave if he wants to?

Horses leave their handlers for a variety of reasons: they may not understand they are supposed to stay; they may not like the handler; or there may be something more interesting around, such as food or another horse. It isn't a bad thing when a horse leaves—it's just feedback. It's up to you, his partner, to work out why he left and what he did before he left so that you can reconnect with him before his feet follow his thoughts.

If he does wander off, just go with him. You're working in a small space, anyway, so use your recall cue for him to come back to you (see p. 102). When he does, don't immediately start work again. Instead, give him scratches, treats, peace—whatever his motivation is—and finish for the day. If you start work immediately, he won't feel motivated to return to you so quickly next time.

EXERCISE 33

Walking Through Pole Patterns

WHAT IT IS

Back in *Exercise 15: Stepping Through Poles* (p. 61), you looked at asking a horse to make his way through piles of poles or branches. Now you're going to build patterns that are made up of corridors of poles with twists and turns. Your aim is to keep the horse inside the pole corridor without touching or stepping over the poles. If you haven't got enough poles, you can use long ropes to outline a path, or if you have an arena with sand footing, you can draw patterns on the surface. I've even built small patterns using marker cones with hazard tape between them, so do use your imagination here.

The patterns can be very simple, from just two poles creating a corridor right up to the "S" bend that is used in competitive

33 A Make sure your horse is confident about walking through a pole corridor first.

Horse Agility. The "S" bend is formed by placing poles on the ground so they form a wide corridor in the shape of the letter "S." The corridor can be very wide to start with, but as the horse becomes more athletic and practiced, make it much more narrow so the turns become tighter and more difficult to navigate. As you develop the patterns, you are looking for turns to the right and to the left, as well as tight turns, so that the horse has to really use all four quarters to get around the corners. This is where you, the handler, need to think about steering. The horse does not know that he is supposed to stay inside the corridor and not touch the poles. If you do not direct him, he will take the easy route and just step out. You could raise the poles but that defeats the object of this exercise, which is you learning to steer your horse wherever you want him to go.

33 B & C Then you can start to make simple patterns to walk through (B). In a more complex maze, Becky looks to move Archie's right hind foot, which needs to step around the end of the inside pole (C).

HOW TO DO IT

Build a simple two-pole corridor. Make it wide and lead the horse through. Some horses may find this difficult, refusing to walk into the corridor or rushing once they are between the poles. You may need to make the corridor very wide to start with. Once you know he is happy walking through two wide-apart poles, you can start to make the corridor narrower. Look for the moment when he tells you the corridor is too narrow and help him by making it a little wider. You and the horse are working together, so listen for his feedback (figs. 33 A–C).

Once you've got the corridor solid, you can start to extend the pattern by adding two more poles and creating an L-shaped corridor. Keep it wide to start with and think about where his feet need to be to get around the corner without him feeling he needs to step out. Walk the pattern in both

directions and be interested if he finds one way easy and the other way tricky.

Now that you've got the "L" going smoothly, you can start to add pole corridors in all directions in a zigzag or a "U" shape. Have fun; see how intricate these mazes can be.

WHAT IF

My advice is to keep these patterns really wide to begin as you and your horse work out how to do this. The most common fault I see is that people forget there are two ends to a horse! They pull the front end round the corner and forget that the back end needs to go around the corner, too. An extreme example of this is when people lead their horse through a narrow gap and turn too soon, resulting in the horse catching his hip on the side of the gap. The back end needs to be directed too, so once you've got the front end round the corner, turn your attention to steering the back end.

Don't worry if it's all a bit chaotic at the start, with poles being stepped over, trodden on, and knocked. This is just feedback. Note what you did, or didn't do, for this to happen, and do something different next time.

Try not to repeat the same pattern over and over. Yes, the horse will learn it and soon be able to do it perfectly, but when you change the pattern, you'll have to start all over again and teach him the new pattern. Remember, the aim of this exercise is to learn to steer your horse's feet where you want them to go.

EXERCISE 34
Lining Up to a Mounting Block

WHAT IT IS

Asking your horse to stand perfectly still in a designated place is enormously important. I try not to tie my horses up unless I absolutely have to, so I spend some time showing them where and how I want them to stand. It is so important that the horse stands still at a mounting block when you are about to get on or you can get hurt. When I see people launching themselves from a mounting block onto a moving horse, it really worries me.

This is not a book on troubleshooting, but if you have a horse that won't stand still when you want to get on, you need to find out why. Is he hurting? Maybe he doesn't know he has to stand still. But when a horse constantly moves away from the block as you prepare to get on, it needs investigation. Ask yourself: what is he trying to tell me?

When you don't have a mounting block, any solid box, strong stool, or similar item that you can easily step up onto will do. All you want is to be able to go from standing on the ground beside him to being above his eyeline, looking down on him.

For the purposes of this exercise, we are going to assume that your horse is not in pain and that he simply doesn't know that he is supposed to stand still when you get on. You aren't actually going to get on here, but you are going to pretend you are. You may want to put your horse's saddle on, but you don't have to, and you'll only need a halter and lead rope on the horse, not his bridle.

HOW TO DO IT

Lead your horse to the mounting block, and position him so the stirrup is level with the mounting block, ready for you to step into it. You will still be on the ground at this point and not on the block, which comes later. Be accurate and particular about the exact spot you want him to stand, because you want him to learn that *this* is the place you need him to walk to and wait. Make a fuss of him, treat him, give him a scratch— whatever he likes, and let him know that when he stands in that exact place, good things will happen. Repeat this same exercise a number of times.

Once he's content standing there, I want you to start moving around him (figs. 34

A–C). Walk round his back end (if it's safe to do so) and appear on the other side. You want him to remain still while you move.

Next you can start stepping up onto the mounting block. I suggest you just step up and down quickly to start with, so he hasn't got time to move, and reward him. Gradually make those steps up onto the block become small "Waits" where you remain on the block for longer lengths of time. Always let him know that he's doing everything right with lots of praise.

After a time, you will find your horse enjoys standing at the block while you move around and step up onto the block because it means good things for him.

WHAT IF

Should your horse move, put him back in the correct spot, but don't reward him right away. This is because if you do, he might think you actually *want* him to move around. So often, in this particular exercise, we give what Mark Rashid, a gentle horseman and a great author of many books on horsemanship, calls an "inadvertent reward." By this he means you might think you are rewarding the horse for standing still, but the horse thinks he is being rewarded for moving around.

Here is a great example of the inadvertent reward: The horse stands still at the block, the rider

34 A–C Libby is in a good position for Carol to get on if she wanted to ride. Never move the mounting block to the horse because sometimes you won't be able to move it (A). Libby is happy to stand in position at the mounting block while Carol leaves. Carol can walk around without Libby feeling she needs to move (B). Mounting blocks come in all shapes and sizes (C)!

steps onto the block, and the horse moves away. The rider gets off the block, repositions the horse, gives him a rub or a treat, and steps up onto the block. The horse moves away again. I've seen this go on for what seems like hours. Be very aware of what you actually are marking as correct behavior in the horse.

The easiest way to avoid this scenario is to get good at moving your horse around while you remain on the mounting block. It's not always easy, I know, but I use a long lead rope so I can move the horse around without stepping down. If your horse is very active, be careful he doesn't pull you off the block. You can learn the skills needed to reposition him while standing still on the ground first, then on a much lower block, thus refining your skills from a safer height. Once you have these skills, you can position the horse without stepping down. Every time he stands in that exact position with you *on* the block, reward him—scratch him, give him a treat, let him know that he got the right answer.

And one last note to riders: what is the first thing you do when you get on and have your hand on the reins and feet in the stirrups? Sit still, absolutely still, for as long as you want to. The horse must wait until *you* are ready to move off; then you're ready to ride.

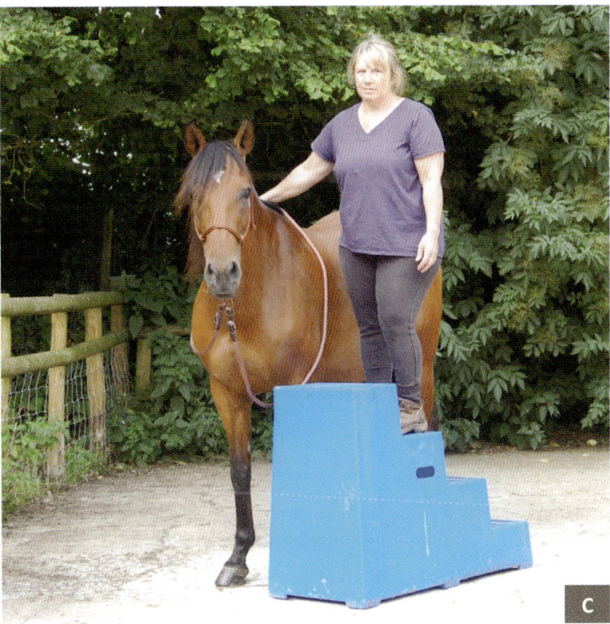

Stepping into a Hula Hoop

I make my own using a length of water pipe bent around into a circle, joined using a short piece of stick or smaller-diameter water pipe pushed into each end.

WHAT IT IS

This is a real exercise in trust. When I first devised this obstacle for Horse Agility Club competitions, I thought it would be easy. How wrong I was!

All you need is a standard hula hoop.

HOW TO DO IT

Place the hoop on the ground and ask the horse to step into it with his front feet and stand still—all without touching the hoop (figs. 35A–D).

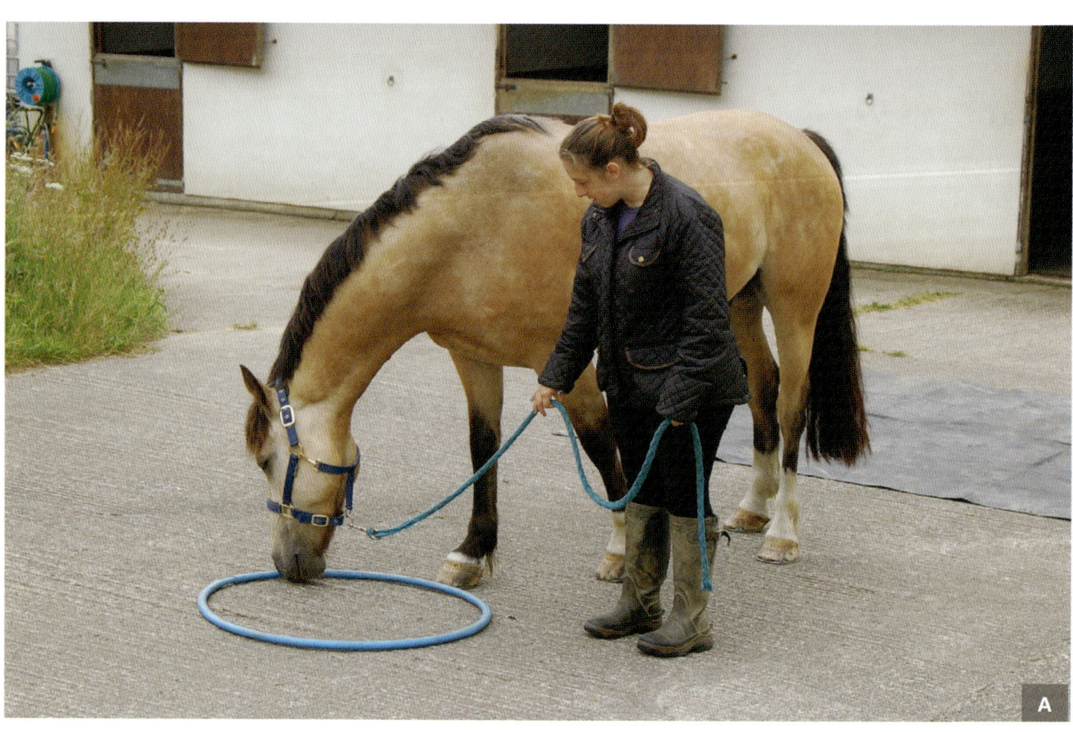

WHAT IF

It sounds so simple, but it is one of the most challenging obstacles in Horse Agility competitions. Some horses refuse to step in, while others just trample all over the hoop.

Let's look at the horse who refuses to step into the hoop: I believe the horse sees that circle as a "hole." Even though the outside ground may be exactly the same surface as the inside, the line of the hoop's circle seems to create a threshold that he doesn't want to cross. The simplest way round this is to open up the hoop until it forms something like a semicircle. Ask him to walk through this space and over the opened hoop until he's comfortable, then ask him to stop in the semicircular space. Once he can do this, you can start to close up the hoop until it forms a complete circle the horse is happy to step into.

But what about the horse that just tramples all over the hoop?

I suggest you go back to *Exercise 14: Moving the Feet* (p. 59) and look at moving his feet individually. You might also find *Exercise 20: Backing Up Over a Pole with the Front Feet* (p. 77) useful in helping the horse lift his feet. Make a mark inside the hoop, focus on one front

35 A & B Breeze loves to investigate any new toys (A). Teri raises the lead rope so Breeze can lift his feet up and into the hoop without touching it (B).

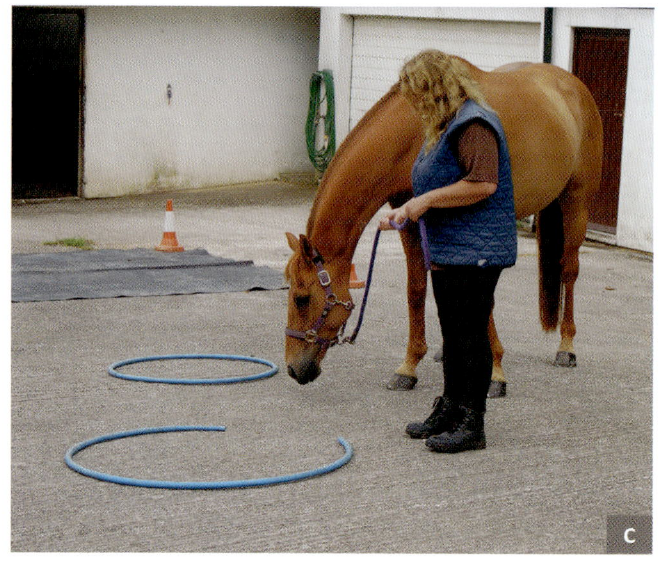

35 C & D Memphis found stepping into a hoop very difficult, so we opened up one of the hoops for him (C). He was much happier with hoop open; we slowly closed the gap as he realized it was safe to step into the middle (D).

foot stepping onto that mark, and get good at directing the feet to where you want them to go. Remember, the horse does not know he's not supposed to touch the hoop, so do let him know when he gets the right answer.

Once the horse is confidently stepping in with his front feet, you can have a go with the hind feet. Good luck!

EXERCISE 36
Turns-on-the-Forehand and Haunches

WHAT IT IS

In *Exercises 12* and *13: Moving the Hind End Around* and *Moving the Front End Around* (pp. 54 and 57), you looked at moving each end of the horse independently. In those exercises, you were only looking for one or two steps, but suppose you want to make a quarter-turn or even a full turn-on-the-forehand or haunches? You need to think about what's happening to the feet you want to keep still. If the horse doesn't move those feet at all, he'll end up in a twist with the "still" feet drilling themselves into the ground. This isn't easy, or physically good for the horse because it puts a lot of stress on his joints.

36 A Lesley askes Daisy to tip her nose toward her and step over (A).

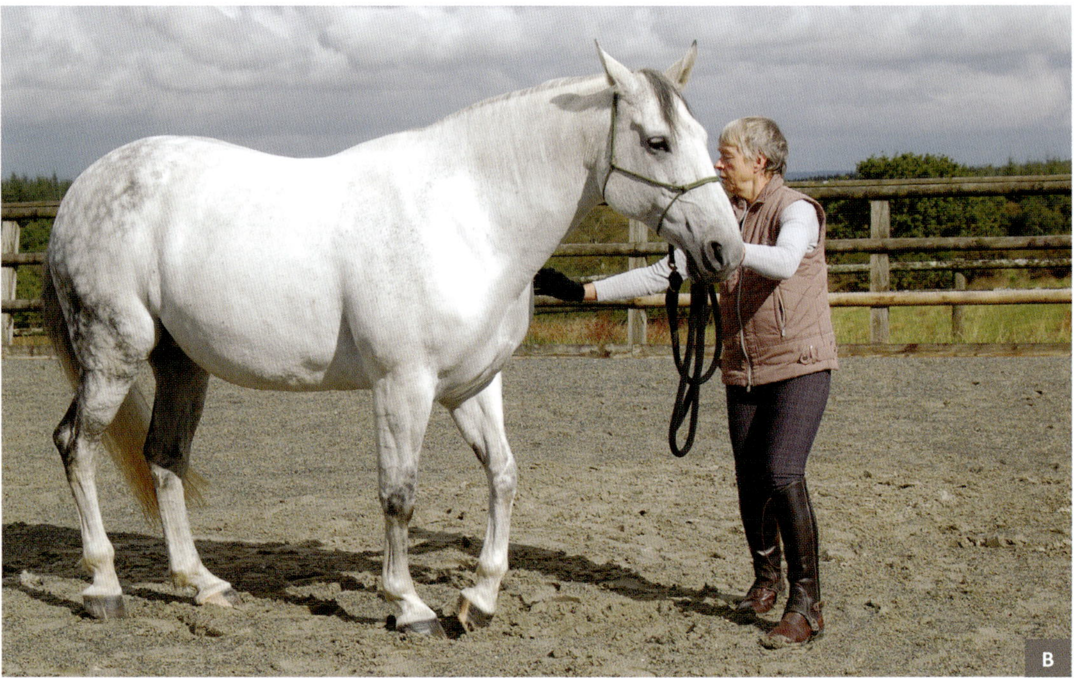

36 B & C All Daisy's feet are "loose" (not "drilled to the ground"), which is good at this level. It would be better if Daisy's nose was tipped a little away from Lesley as she is asked to step her forehand over (B) so she tries again with a much better position for the nose when Daisy's forehand is asked step away (C).

The ultimate aim in this exercise is to direct your horse to do a turn while the feet you want to keep still move *just enough* to prevent any twisting or drilling into the ground. If you could cause those feet to lift up and down without moving away from one spot, you would have a perfect movement. And all in perfect rhythm, of course!

This is what you are heading for, but to start with, of course, all sorts of other things are going to happen. When you move the forehand over, the hind feet might move about all over the place; or perhaps one or both hind feet will dig a hole in the ground as your horse turns. It will get better.

HOW TO DO IT

Just like all the other exercises, we need to break this one down into small achievable tasks:

C

If you start at the front end and ask the horse to step his front end over a step or two (turn-on-the-haunches), you need to notice what the hind feet do and work on that (figs. 36 A–C). When the horse is moving those hind feet toward you as the front end goes away, the horse is essentially swiveling around his middle. This is *not* what you're looking for. We want the hind feet to stay in the same place while the front end steps over. I find the easiest way to help the horse here is to rock his weight back onto his hindquarters *before* I ask him to take a step over with his front feet. At this stage, I'm not too worried about the number of steps, I just don't want the hindquarters stepping toward me or away from me (it is okay if he takes a step back to rearrange his feet, as it's much more important for those feet to stay "loose" and movable and take the weight off the forehand).

When you start this exercise, don't think too big—one perfectly soft step is far better than a jumble of good and bad steps all mixed in together. Each step should feel as though the horse is on wheels, moving around. Remember, you're trying to help the horse understand what you need him to do, so reward often and always stop when it's good.

When you move the hind end around the front (turn-on-the-forehand), you'll find the same thing happening to the front end. It will start to move toward you as the horse swivels around his middle. You don't want the horse drifting forward, so using a fence or wall here might help: face him into the fence before you ask the hind end to step over. Of course, he may want to adjust his front feet, and at this stage, I'm quite

happy if those feet move. It shows he's loose in the shoulders and not drilling his feet into the ground.

This can be a very athletic and demanding skill for some horses, especially when they are young without their muscles and skeleton fully formed yet, and with older horses that might be a bit stiff. Put yourself in their position—if you haven't been to an exercise class for a long time, you'll probably find it hard work if you suddenly join the advanced group.

WHAT IF

Look for a little and reward often. The feeling of the movement being "loose" and soft is much more important than accuracy at this level. Don't get too hung up in keeping the feet still at one end while you move the other—you'll do that next.

EXERCISE 37
Refining the Turns-on-the-Forehand and Haunches

WHAT IT IS

You're now going to start to be a bit more particular about what's happening to the feet you want to remain still. You do this by creating a space to put these feet into so you can be honest about how much they are moving. You will need to have looked at *Exercises 12* and *13: Moving the Hind End Around* and *Moving the Front End Around* (pp. 54 and 57), and have worked through *Exercises 35* and *36: Stepping into a Hula Hoop* and *Turns-on-the-Forehand and Haunches* (pp. 122 and 125) to ensure the foundation skills are solid before you attempt this.

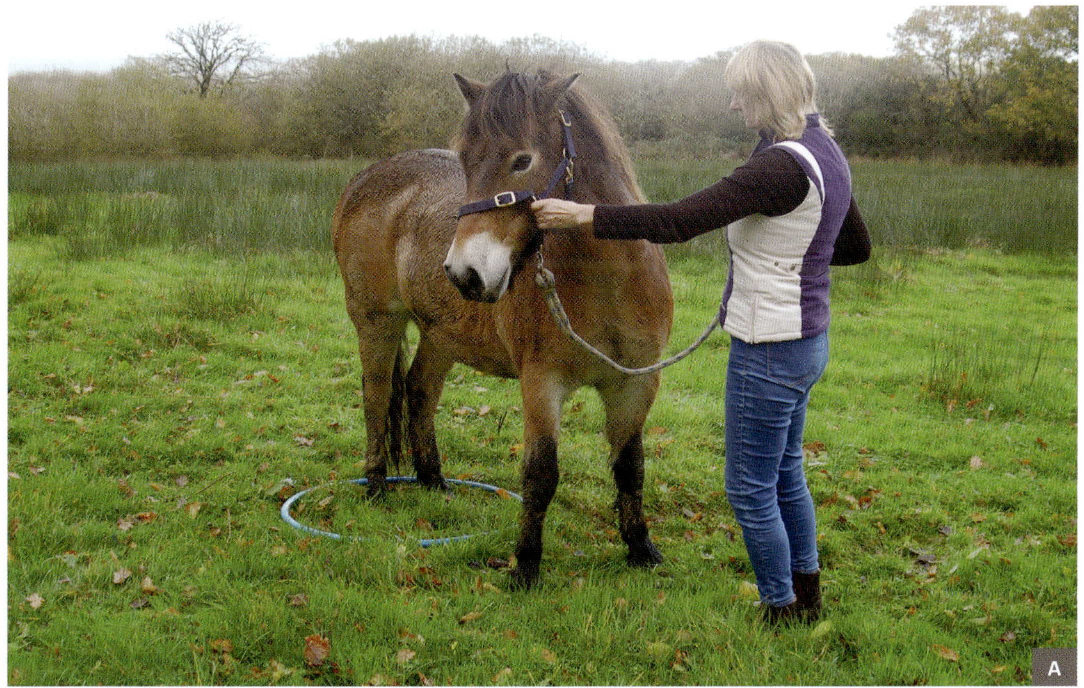

37 A I'm asking Ricky, very quietly, to step his front end over without stepping out of the hoop with his hind feet.

37 B Then I move his hind end away without him stepping out of the hoop with his front feet.

HOW TO DO IT

Using a hula hoop, or a circle drawn on the ground with sand or shavings, ask your horse to stand with his hind feet in it.

Now ask him to move his forehand away from you (fig. 37 A). What do his hind feet do? Stay still or begin to move around? If they stay still, ask him to free them up by stepping back, but not so much that he steps out of the circle. All you're doing is repositioning him so his body is not twisted. If he steps out of the circle with his hind feet, ask him to step back into it. Then, ask the front end to move over again. Repeat until you feel you've had one good step, then stop. This is a very complex exercise and should be treated with care.

Next, try doing a turn-on-the-forehand. Ask him to put his front feet in the circle and step around with his hind feet (fig. 37 B). The front end will probably move, but as long as the front feet stay in the circle, I am happy with that in the beginning. If the feet step out of the hoop, replace them and ask again.

WHAT IF

This is a long process; don't overwork it in one session. Experiment with how you are asking the horse to move and how you might need to change the way you are asking to get the desired result. The position of your hand, for instance, could have a huge influence on which of the horse's feet will move first. Fiddle around with moving his feet and see how you can influence them.

EXERCISE 38
Walking Through a Curtain of Streamers

WHAT IT IS

It's highly unlikely that out on a ride or at a show you will encounter such a thing as a frame with streamers to walk through, but this is a fun skill that builds trust and confidence in the horse and helps you learn more about how your horse learns.

HOW TO DO IT

You will need to find or build a frame from which you can hang a lot of streamers or ribbons. A doorway can work for the frame, but do make sure it is wide enough for your horse to go through with plenty of room on each side in case he rushes.

For the streamers, you can buy special fly curtains, which are cheap and quick to set up, or you can use an old shower curtain or bedsheet cut into strips. The aim is for the streamers to look like a solid wall with no gaps—they need to completely fill the frame so there is no space at the

38 A Daisy was happy walking through the curtain with all the streamers tied back, so Lesley dropped one streamer.

edge of the door for the horse to sneak through.

Don't start with all the streamers hanging down; tie all of them out of the way so that the horse can see right through. Some horses will still find this very scary, so give your horse time to examine the whole frame and curtain. These early

38 B & C As Daisy became comfortable with one streamer, more were released to hang down (B). The mare is fine pushing her way through all the streamers when they hang down to form a "wall" (C).

investigations are really important to him; give him the time he needs with no pressure to walk through.

Using the safety measures you looked at in *Exercise 16: Passing Through a Narrow Gap* (p. 63), ask your horse to wait while you pass through the curtain frame; then, standing well to the side, ask him to come to you (figs. 38 A–C). No pressure—just a simple request to join you. He might stroll through, hurry through in a panic, or just freeze and refuse to move. If he does the latter, wait. You can have expectation in your attitude that you want him to walk through, but no more than that. However, if you just relax and stand there waiting, he might

well wait you out, so keep your energy up, *expecting* him to make some attempt to walk through. It's really important to stay out of the way while you're asking him to come through because he may hurry, and in his panic, run into you.

When he does think about walking through, he could just rock forward or reach out with his nose. Don't pull on the lead rope because it will immediately cause him to feel trapped, and he'll pull back away from the curtain. Reward him for a rock or reach, let him know that it was a great try, and ask again.

You need to have the feeling in you that you have all day, all week, *all year* to wait for him. I like to get three tries at having him come through; then, after the third try, I go back to the horse and lead him away from the curtain. I might go and do something else just to give him a bit of breathing space, and then come back to the exercise.

Once he's gone through the curtain frame while it is tied open with no streamers hanging down, repeat that walk through until he's perfectly happy. Then, drop one streamer. Most horses accept this, but you do get the occasional one who goes back to refusing to walk through. You know what you had to do last time to be successful, so just repeat that. Start to drop more streamers, maybe one or two at a time, leading the horse through each time so he's comfortable at each level until he is pushing his way through all the streamers without hesitation.

WHAT IF

Do go slowly on this one—the more time you take early on, the more comfortable your horse will become. I want my horses to become brave and thoughtful, not more scared of me and the obstacles I present to them. I want my horses to think and work it out for themselves. You could use a whip or flag to drive the horse through, but that gains you nothing but a horse that's more scared of you than the obstacle.

Thunderstorm

The following exercises include a lot of the skills you have picked up in the previous lessons in this book. They are intricate and can be time-consuming, so don't be too worried about stopping in a good place and returning to the exercise later. With some, you need to work out the individual steps in order to be successful. Make a list of all the skills you will need, refresh them with your horse by going back to earlier lessons in the book, then work out where you need to start.

In this section I will not be dividing the exercises into *What, How,* and *What If.* I will describe the exercise, then offer some suggestions on where you can find the information to complete it where it appears earlier in this book.

EXERCISE 39
The Hula Hoop Square

You need four hula hoops for this exercise, but if you haven't got enough, use a lead rope laid on the ground in a circle, or draw circles with shavings. Arrange the hoops on the ground as if they are the corners of a square. The sides of the square can be about two horse-lengths long to give you enough space.

Start at any hoop and walk your horse into it (*Exercise 35: Stepping into a Hula Hoop,* p. 122) and halt with his front feet in that hoop. You are now going to ask him to do a turn-on-the-forehand (*Exercise 12: Moving the Hind End Around,* p. 54) by moving his hindquarters until he is facing the next hoop on the square. He then walks to that next hoop and halts in it with his hind feet (figs. 39 A & B). Then ask him to do a turn-on-the-haunches (*Exercise 13: Moving the Front End Around,* p. 57) until he is facing the next hoop in the square.

39 A & B After a turn-on-the-fore-hand with the front feet remaining in the hoop, we prepare to walk to the next hoop (A). At the next corner, we stopped with Ricky's hind feet in the shavings hoop and made a turn-on-the-haunches before preparing to walk to the next hoop (B).

He walks to that third hoop and stops with his front feet in it. You then ask him to move his hind end around until he is facing the fourth and final hoop, which he walks to and halts with his hind feet in it. He turns on his hind end to face the first hoop of the sequence. (For riders, this is a great exercise under saddle, too.)

You can increase the challenge by saying you're only allowed one touch at each hoop, or no touches at all!

EXERCISE 40
The Counted Walk

The Counted Walk is a way of moving each foot in the sequence of walk in a ticking clock rhythm. You know your horse can walk, but can you ask each foot to step and halt before the next foot in the sequence gets going?

First of all, you need to know the footfall sequence of the walk: right hind, right front, left hind, left front. You can start with the left hind, of course, followed by the left front, but the main thing to remember is that the hind foot steps first, then the front foot on that same side steps next, almost as if it's stepping out of the way of the hind foot coming forward (figs. 40 A–D).

I thoroughly recommend you get down on all fours and walk this through. My classical riding coach, Perry Wood, made us all get off our horses, get down on all fours, and "walk," "trot," and "canter" so we felt the sequence of the feet. It really helped me understand how a

40 A & B Left hind steps forward (A), left fore steps forward (B).

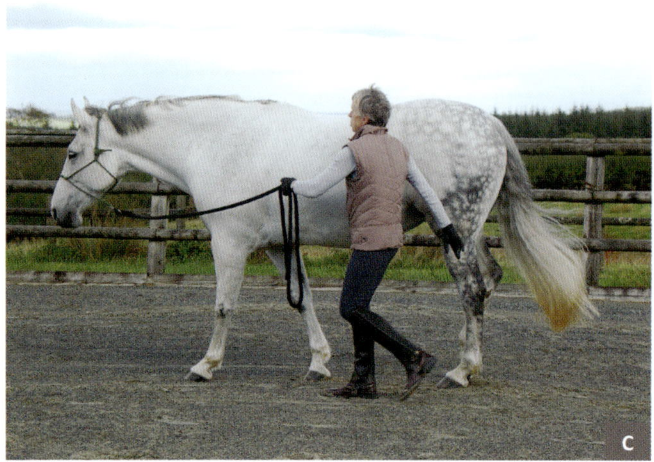

40 C & D Right hind steps forward (C), right fore steps forward (D).

four-legged animal moves in each gait and where his feet need to be as he changes from one gait to another. It helped me remember the sequence, too.

This exercise is to walk the horse in a step-by-step rhythm in a straight line. You're aiming for a rhythmic walk, counting like a ticking clock; right hind (tick); right front (tock); left hind (tick); left front (tock). The horse at this stage might look rather mechanical, but as you improve the rhythm (and increase the speed), the horse will gather himself and begin to flow. Even though the steps are slow and measured, there will be forward energy in the movement.

SUGGESTIONS

Do not start with the final part of the Challenge. Understand the walk sequence, and get the order consistently starting with the hind foot moving first (*Exercise 14: Moving the Feet* may help you—p. 59); only then start to work on the rhythm. Do not focus on the final goal; be patient and really support the horse as he tries to work out what you need him to do.

EXERCISE 41
All Together Now!

If you've had a go at *Exercise 40: The Counted Walk* (p. 137), you're getting to know how to move each foot independently. In this exercise, you're going to play around with moving the feet to a very specific point that creates quite an unnatural stance for the horse (figs. 41 A & B). If

41 A & B A great start getting all four feet in a small space (A) and a raised platform where all four feet are positioned into a different small space (B).

you have a look at *Exercise 14: Moving the Feet* (p. 59), there are some tips there on how to get started moving feet one by one.

You will need a small mat or a hula hoop. Be aware that the hoop can be more difficult to use because, when the horse touches it and moves it around, you have to keep adjusting where you want the feet to go. If the horse, or you, find this particularly challenging, make the mat and the hoop quite big. What you are attempting to do is get the horse to stand with all four feet on the mat.

As with all these THUNDERSTORM EXERCISES, this takes time and patience and tests all the skills you have at your disposal. Is it just a trick? Well, yes. Anything you do with a horse that causes him to perform an unnatural act for reward is a trick.

Walk Fast, Walk Slow

All this work on the ground is about good leading. Can you lead your horse on a loose lead rope without pulling on him or him pulling on you? You looked at leading in *Exercises 9* and *11: Easy Leading* and *Dancing Together* (pp. 43 and 51), where you started to synchronize with your horse and he with you. This exercise is testing these skills. You need to be able to walk freely beside your horse here, preferably in a straight line (it's easier!), but it can be done on a circle. It sounds simple, but I think you'll be amazed at how it really shows up in our leading skills.

Set two markers 50 feet (15 meters) apart in a straight line, but it doesn't have to be that distance if you're limited on space.

42 A Lesley is adjusting her stride and body language to walk slowly.

141

42 B Lesley picks up her energy to get a good strong walk with Daisy.

Place another marker at the middle point of this distance. At the first marker, walk at your normal pace to the middle marker. Halt. Start to walk very slowly (as if in slow motion) to the next marker (fig. 42 A—note: here the markers are not in view). Don't stop. Both your feet and the horse's feet must keep moving throughout. When you reach the end marker, turn and walk as fast as you possibly can without breaking into a trot back to the beginning (fig. 42 B).

I often suggest people video themselves doing this—it's so easy these days with our phones. Did you retain the leading position? Did the rope stay the same shape, nice and loose? Was the slow walk slow enough? This sounds like such a simple exercise, but I think it's one of the harder ones in this book. It's a bit like dressage—when it's done well, it looks easy!

EXERCISE 43
One Pole, One Step at a Time

You only need one pole for this exercise, and I suggest you find a way to stop the pole from rolling, or use a half-round rail. Note this needs to be something the horse has to lift his feet up and over—a lead rope on the ground would not be thick enough.

To complete this exercise, you are going to ask your horse to walk over the pole, one step at a time. You've explored this idea of moving the feet individually a lot through these *Rainy Day Exercises.* Have a look back

43 A Timing is everything here: be ready to stop the foot as soon as it is lifted up to step over the pole. Leave it too late and the other foot will have started to move. Lesley's timing is slightly off in Photo A. She wanted Daisy to halt with just her left foot over the pole, but the right foreleg is already lifting to step over. It takes a lot of concentration to get that foot to stop where you want it to.

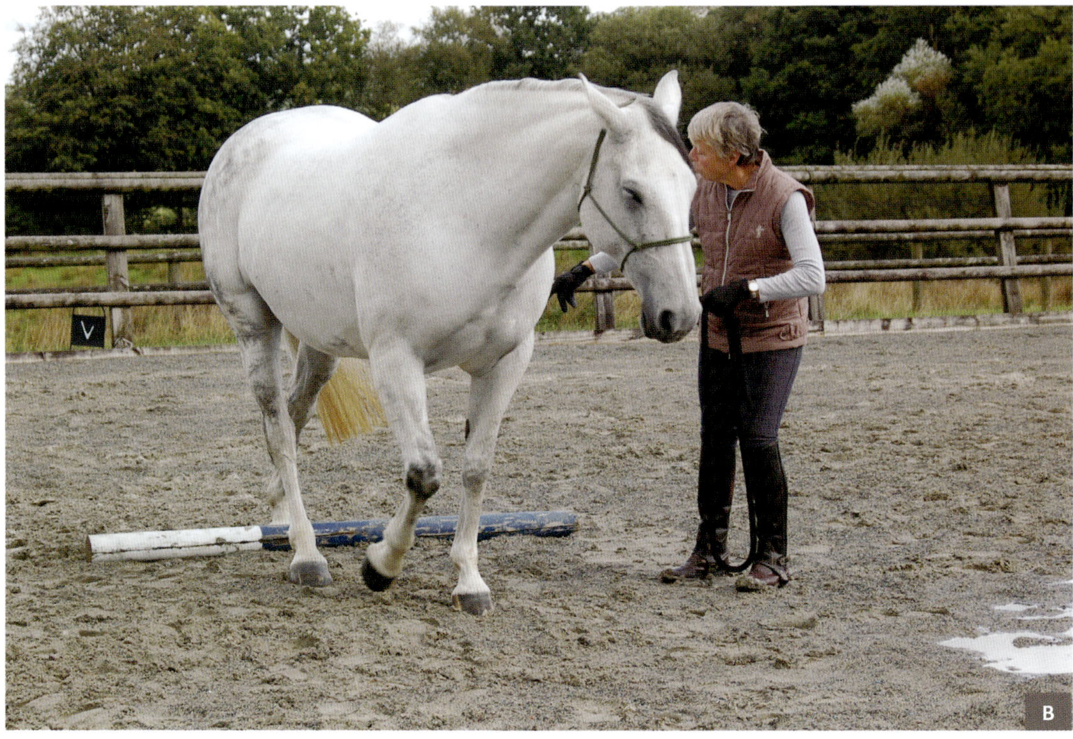

43 B Lesley asks Daisy to halt before stepping over the pole with her left hind foot.

at *Exercises 14: Moving the Feet, 15: Stepping Through Poles, 20: Backing Up Over a Pole with the Front Feet,* and *21: Backing Up Over a Pole with All Four Feet* (pp. 59, 61, 77, and 80). They all have helpful ideas.

Lead your horse to the pole and ask him to step one front foot over it, halt, and count to three. Ask for the second front foot to step over and count to three, and so on, until all four feet have stepped up and over the pole. The aim is for the feet not to touch the pole.

When you have done that perfectly, try backing all four feet over. Good luck!

EXERCISE 44
Walking the Pole

I like finding exercises that involve simple equipment and really test the skills of the handler, and in this exercise all you need is a single pole. In all the obstacle work I do, the actual equipment is not important. It's about the handler's ability to tell the horse how and where to move his feet, and in this exercise, nothing is truer! What you are attempting to do here is to ask the horse to walk along, from one end to the other, straddling the pole with it under his body between his front and hind legs (figs. 44 A–C). This is about foot control, so *Exercises 12: Moving the Hind End Around, 13: Moving the Front End Around,* and *14: Moving the Feet* (pp. 54, 57, and 59) will be immensely useful here.

The main problems start when the handler simply assumes the horse knows where

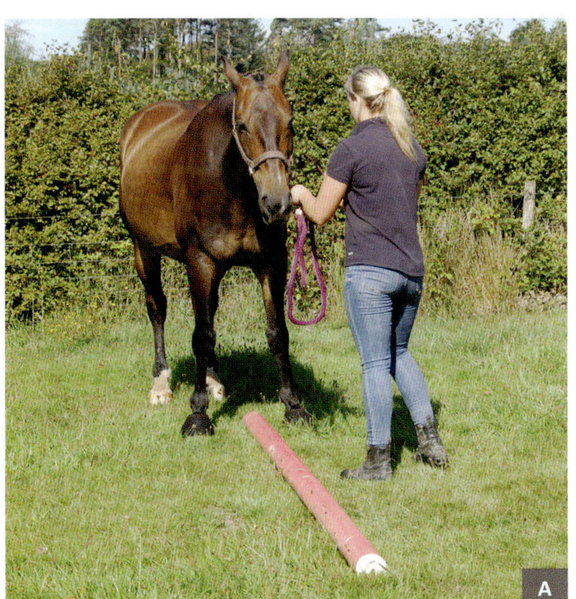

44 A & B A good start; the pole is just between Archie's front feet (A). The back feet need to be carefully positioned here to take the next step (B).

44 C Nearly there!

he is supposed to put his feet. Think like a horse here! In an open space, why would a horse possibly choose to do this? It has no meaning for him when there is an easier path to walk. Directing his feet is the only way to achieve success.

Most people find moving the front feet easy; it's when they try to direct the back feet that they lose control of the front feet, and then the horse steps on the pole, gets concerned, and can even panic. Always, in these potential panic situations, I tell people to *slow down*. Get one step, relax, and reward to mark that correct movement so the horse knows he is going in the right direction.

The first time you try this, you might only get one or two feet in position, but that is a great start. Remember to let the horse know that, too!

EXERCISE 45
Walking the Rope

This is an extension of the previous exercise but much trickier because the horse is quite comfortable stepping all over a rope, unlike not wanting to knock his feet on a hard pole.

Lay a long rope on the ground in a straight line, and, using the same skills as *Exercise 44: Walking the Pole* (p. 145), ask

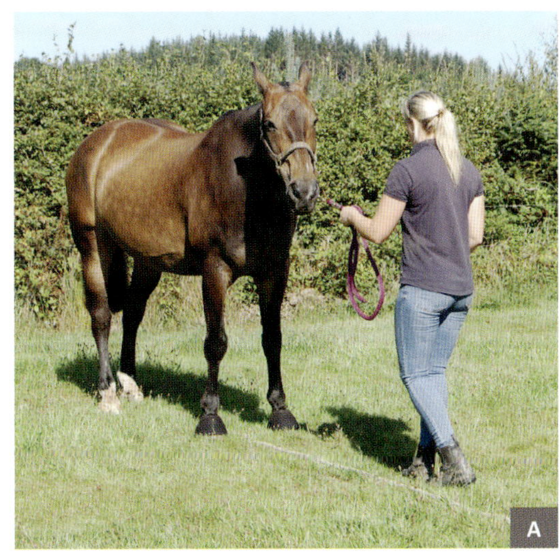

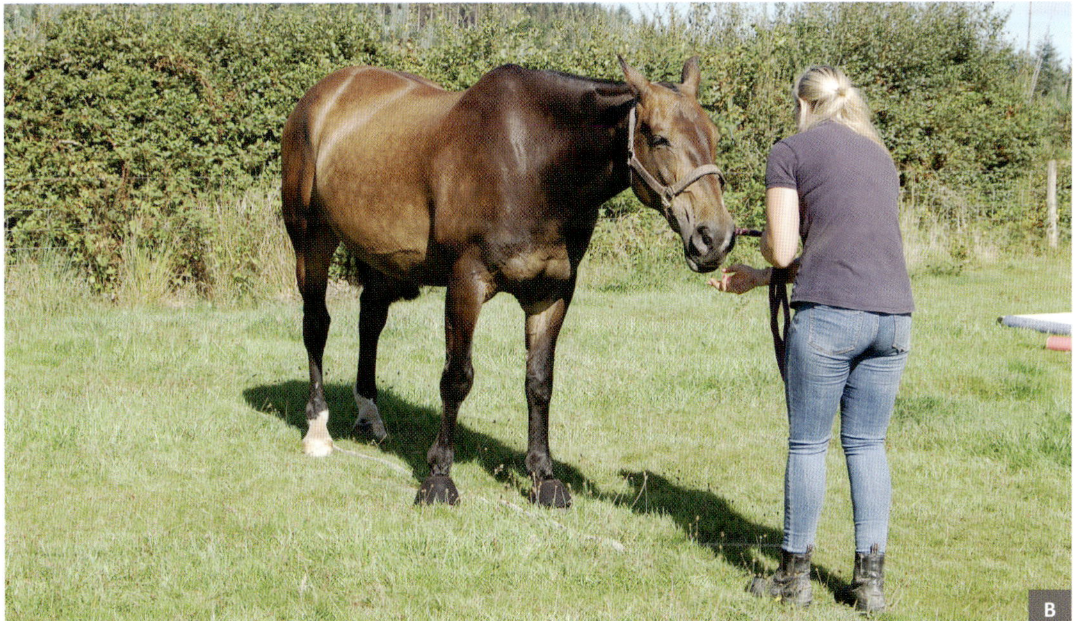

45 A & B Becky is ready to direct those feet to step on each side of the rope (A). She asks the left hind to step forward (B).

45 C She and her horse get a good finish!

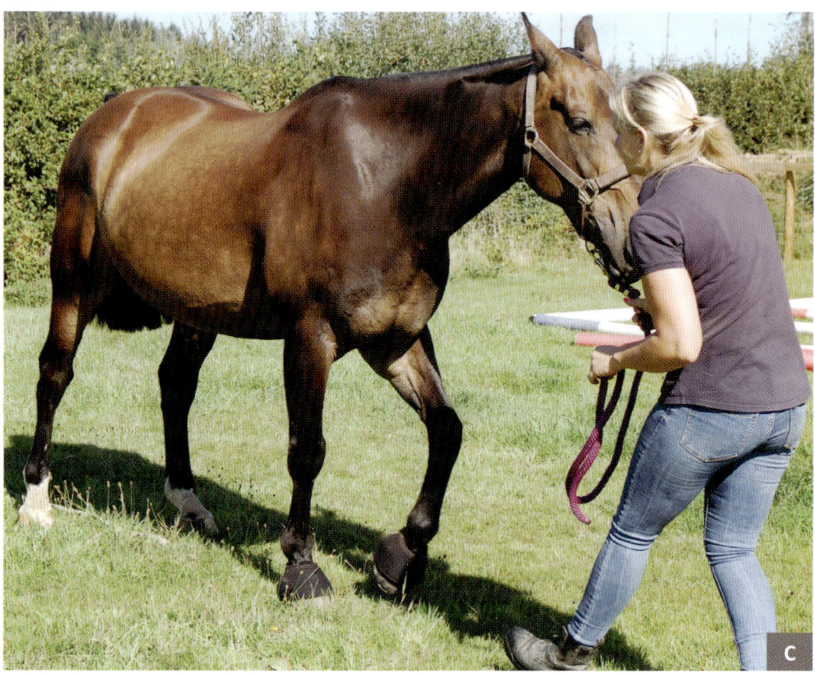

your horse to walk along the rope with his feet on each side (figs. 45 A–C). Can you see how he has complete disregard for the rope? Infuriating, maybe, but also great for practicing your horsemanship patience.

This is a particularly good exercise for being disciplined about stopping when the lesson is going well. We can get so focused on the final goal, we keep going while not noticing that the horse's responses are becoming more and more random. How many times have you gotten to the end of a training session with your horse and wished you'd quit half an hour ago, when things were going well?

Now for an extension to this exercise: my horse Secret (who passed away while I was writing this book) was learning to walk the rope by placing her feet one in front of the other, as if on a tight rope. She almost had it, too. She taught me so much about accurately placing horses' feet, but it was through many, many hours' work between the two of us. If you want to get better at something, you need to practice. There are no shortcuts here, so enjoy the process.

EXERCISE 46
The Circular Weave

This is a most impressive exercise, especially if you can complete it without a lead rope attached. You will need five cones or markers and something to mark the center, where you are going to stand. Set the cones equally distanced in a circle around that center point. You may want the cones to be close to the center at first, then move them out as you become better at this. *Exercises 27: Weaving Through Cones, 28: Send Your Horse Away and Around a Marker,* and *29: The Figure Eight* (pp. 99, 102, and 104) will help you here.

While you stand still, only turning to follow the horse as he moves around you,

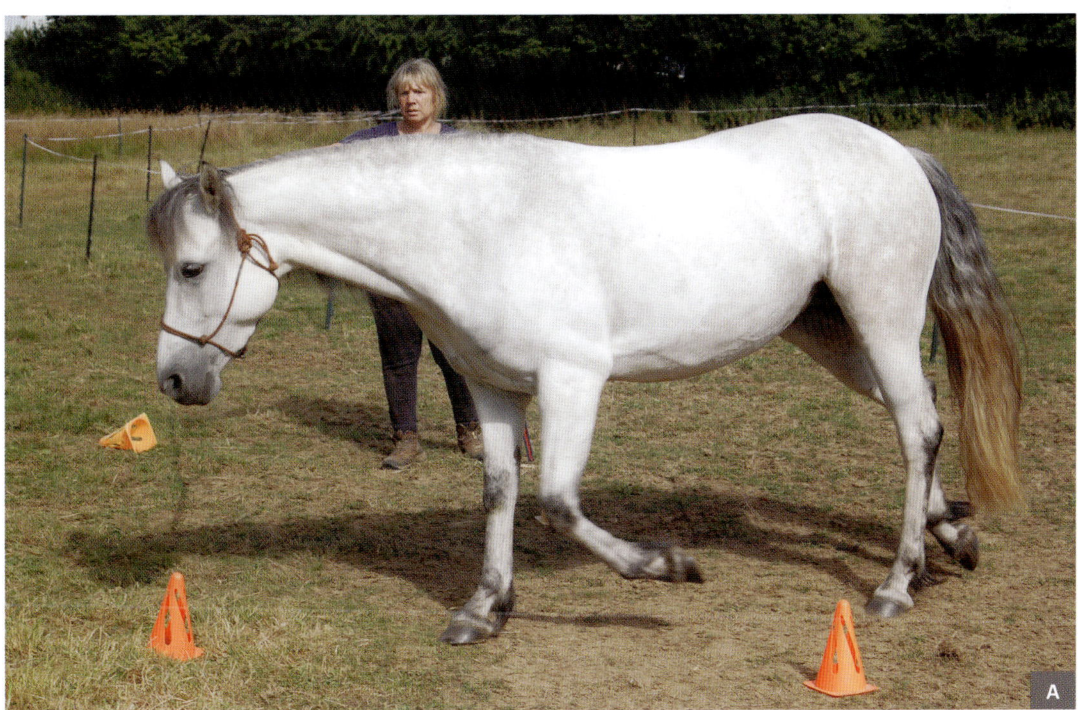

46 A The concentration on Carol's face says it all as she asks Melody to "Go away" around the cone.

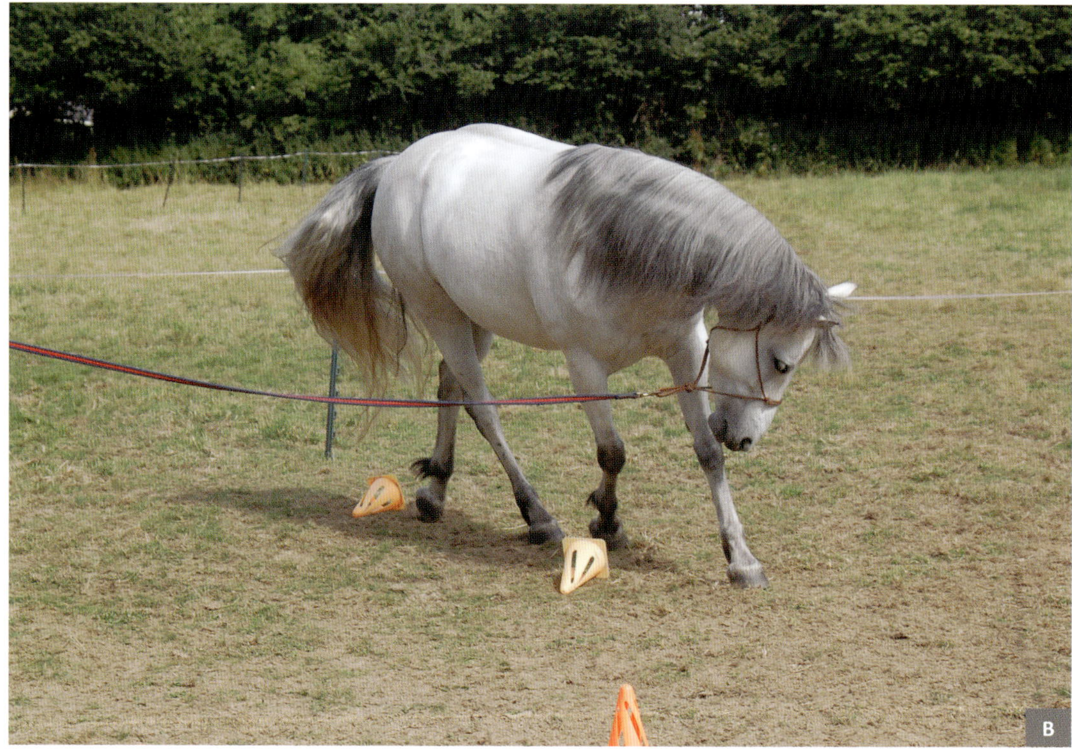

46 B Melody starts to have fun and put her own ideas into the challenge (B). It's like she's thinking, "How many cones can I knock over?"

direct him to weave through the cones evenly and smoothly, coming and going in a wave (figs. 46 A & B). To start with, you might have quite a small circle, as I mentioned, but as you gain skills and confidence, try making the circle much bigger so the horse is working at longer and longer distances from you. Try this in trot and canter, too.

Once you have reached this level of communication with your horse, you will begin to wonder why you ever need to use a lead rope at all.

The Sun Is Shining!

All the exercises you have been working on, whether inside to avoid getting wet or outside when you just can't or don't want to ride, have had a purpose. My one great passion is to get people out of the arena, out of closed spaces, and to really feel the freedom of being able to take their horses anywhere with a lead rope or under saddle. When your horse's legs become your own, when you feel confident that you can get out of a sticky situation because you have the skills to do so, it gives you great courage to explore more, and to do so more often.

Going for a Walk

The wonderful thing about horses—well, one of thousands—is that we don't need to ride them to enjoy their company. Getting good at handling them on the ground is imperative if you are going to go out walking with your horse. At minimum, he needs to know that he must stay with you and trust that in a tricky situation, you are there to support him and get him out of trouble.

This is what all these *Rainy Day Exercises* have been working toward: building skills and trust (figs. 47 A–F).

If you haven't done much hand-walking outside your own property, I suggest you keep that first trip outside very short. You might just go out the gate, look up and down the road, and go back. You don't need to take a long journey; keep it short and interesting. You might know there's a tasty grass bank a little ways away and go to that. Let your horse have a nibble and come home.

When you know there is something potentially scary on the way, avoid it to start

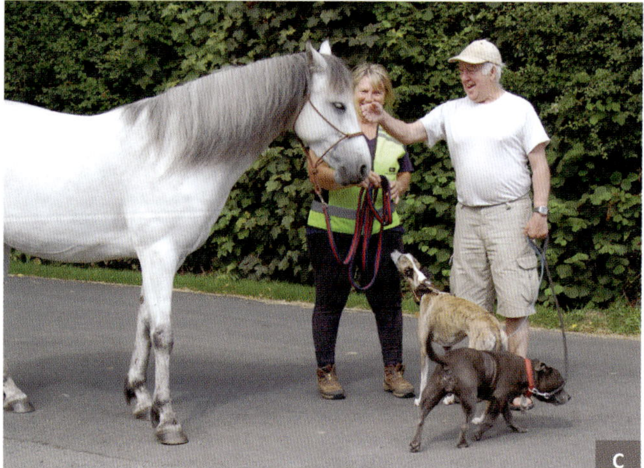

47 A–F A horse living in a domestic environment has to get used to many different types of obstacles (A). Trash day brings its own set of challenges, but here, Melody looks more interested in the grass (B). Meeting friends and dogs (C). Squeezing through the overgrown gateway by the church (D). Visiting the local village shop (E). And finding out what's new (F).

with. Early walks need to build confidence, so be ready to turn in the road when the going is good, and go home. Listen to your horse; he knows well before you do that there's something potentially scary around the next corner. It isn't "giving in" or being a failure to avoid a dangerous situation. It's common sense.

These short forays out are nothing to do with anyone else; they are between you and your horse. Other people may be able to lead or ride their horses for miles. I am happy for them, but you might not be ready for that. Trust yourself and your horse. You both know better than anyone else whether you are ready for a bigger adventure.

Horse Agility

I'm going to put *Horse Agility* here as an exercise because I know how many people have benefited from this amazing nonridden equestrian sport. Started in 2009, The International Horse Agility Club (thehorseagilityclub.com) administers the sport worldwide and publishes monthly obstacle courses, which can be

48 A–D The narrow gap (A), the curtain (B), the corridor of flags and bunting (C), and tight space with road signs (D).

built easily at home. By following the criteria outlined for each obstacle, people can compete by videoing themselves completing the course with their horse and enter competitions without ever having to leave home. The courses range from very simple ones (there are walk-only classes for those who cannot move too quickly) right up to advanced liberty classes (figs. 48 A–D).

All the *Rainy Day Horsemanship* exercises I have described so far in this book will help you develop great skills, not only to get really good at *Horse Agility*, but to develop a safe, trusting relationship with your horse. In *Horse Agility*, the horse is encouraged to think and make decisions about how he is going to react in any given situation. He is not dulled or desensitized, but encouraged to explore and learn about the domestic world around him. This is what this whole book has been about—creating a thinking horse, *not* a machine.

EXERCISE 49
Showing
in Hand

If you are someone who likes to get out and about with your horse, showing in hand is a fun way. You get all the enjoyment of preparing your horse for the show and the challenge of presenting a gleaming, beautifully turned-out horse to the judge (fig. 49). I showed driving ponies for many years, and it would take three days to prepare for each show: one day to clean the harness, one to clean the vehicle, and one to polish and braid the pony. I loved it, so I quite understand why people want to do it.

I see some beautifully turned-out horses and handlers, but their showing skills can often let them down. These *Rainy*

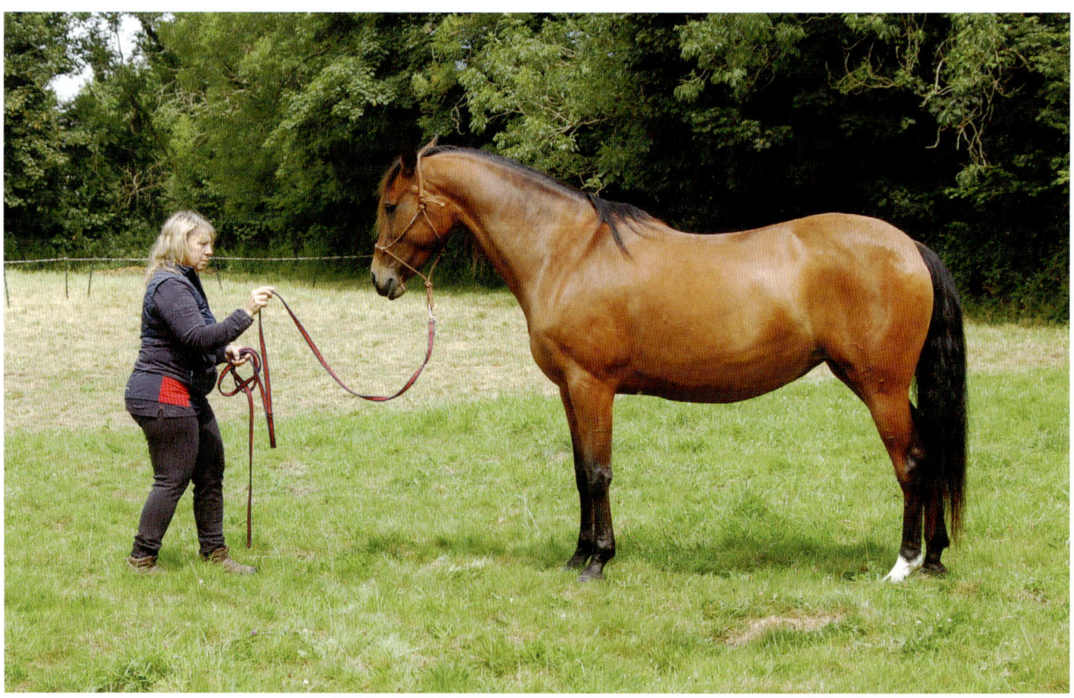

49 A horse that stands well will catch the judge's eye.

Day Horsemanship exercises go a long way to helping you present a better picture to the judge:

- ***Exercise 8: Standing Still* (p. 38)** Waiting to go into the ring or in the line-up before you present to the judge is a moment for you and your horse to recharge your batteries, so that when you need to show off you can really sparkle.

- ***Exercise 11: Dancing Together* (p. 51)** Synchronize with your horse's legs as you walk with him, and get a good, solid trot cue in place so he really picks up a balanced trot to show off his paces.

- ***Exercise 14: Moving the Feet* (p. 59)** You don't want your horse to "slouch" in front of the judge. You can position his feet to present him to his best advantage instead of being out of shape because he has halted in the wrong way.

And think about all those exercises where you came face to face with potentially scary things: tarpaulins, flags, and umbrellas. None will challenge your horse at a show because he's seen them all before.

EXERCISE 50

Lie in the Sun with Your Horse

50 Enjoying the sunshine after a good roll, and having a snooze while friends groom each other. Nothing better than when there's nothing else to do but just be a horse.

Now cut yourself some slack. The rain has gone, the sun is shining, and the horses are out in the pasture doing what horses do. Don't be afraid to go and hang out with them (fig. 50). Don't expect anything; let them just *be*. If they come over to say hello, that's good. If they don't, that's good, too. You're doing your best to understand what they need, and they will know that.

Enjoy.

ACKNOWLEDGMENTS

With grateful thanks to my friends
who helped me with this book.

Becky and Archie

Carol and Melody

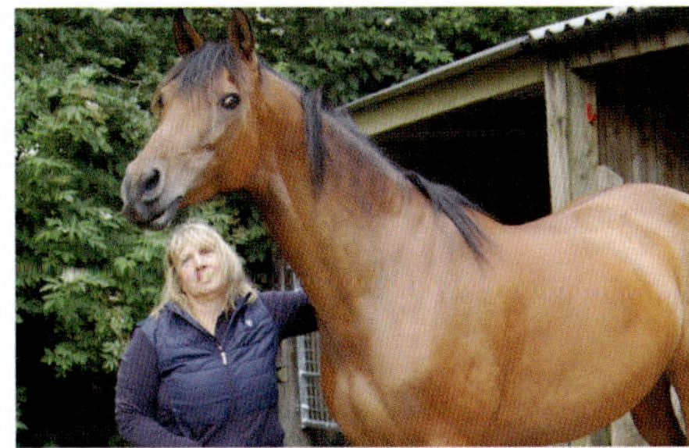

Carol and Libby

Lesley and Daisy

Rachel and Memphis

Teri and Breeze

Ricky, who stepped in at the last minute

Index

Page numbers in italics indicate illustrations.